*Treasured
Friends*

To Nancy,

With love,

Ann Hibbard

♡

Other Books by Ann Hibbard

Treasured Friends

Finding and Keeping True Friendships

Ann Hibbard

Baker Books

A Division of Baker Book House Co
Grand Rapids, Michigan 49516

Published by Baker Books
a division of Baker Book House Company
P.O. Box 6287, Grand Rapids, MI 49516-6287

Paper edition published 1998

Library of Congress Cataloging-in-Publication Data

Hibbard, Ann, 1956–
    Treasured friends : finding and keeping true friendships / Ann Hibbard.
        p.   cm.
    Includes bibliographical references.
    ISBN 0-8010-1150-7 (cloth)
    ISBN 0-8010-5827-9 (paper)
    1. Women—Psychology. 2. Female friendship. 3. Female friendship—Religious aspects. I. Title.
HQ1026.H45   1997
302.3'4—dc21   97-3403

Except as noted, the stories in this book are true. Many of the names, locations, and other minor details have been changed to protect the privacy of those mentioned.

For current information about all releases from Baker Book House, visit our web site:
                    http://www.bakerbooks.com

To
five true friends:
Debbie Bennetch, Linda Garnier, Noreene Janus,
Beth Spring, and Martha Vetter

Contents

Acknowledgments

To the women who shared with me their stories of friendship I owe a tremendous debt. Many of your stories grace the pages of this book.

Once again, I enjoy the honor of publishing with Baker Book House Company. A special thanks to those who presented this project with such zeal: Twila Bennett, Marci De Vries, and Stephen Griffith. Editors Liz Heaney and Melinda Van Engen spurred me on to do better than my best.

Finally, thank you to my greatest cheerleader, my true friend, my daughter, Laura.

*A faithful friend is
a strong defense: and he that
hath found such an one
hath found a treasure.*

Ecclesiasticus 6:14

1   *True Friends*

She captured my heart from the very beginning. I first noticed her in Señor Enriquez's Spanish class as she stood in front of the class giving a recitation. Her gleaming black hair, olive skin, and Mediterranean nose distinguished her from most of my classmates, who were of Scandinavian or German descent. But what attracted me most was her laugh. Her nose crinkled and her eyes danced. I thought, *I want to be her friend. She looks like a lot of fun.*

My instinct proved to be true. Ellen and I became the best of friends, and we laughed together like only junior high school girls can. We both played in the band—Ellen, bass clarinet, and I, alto clarinet. Often I looked up from my music only to see that Ellen had draped locks of her hair across the neck of her bass clarinet to form a long handlebar moustache. She wiggled her eyebrows up and down in her best "Frito Bandito" imitation.

We watched *Star Trek* every night, calling each other up afterward to recite our favorite lines. We wrote science fiction romance stories about being marooned on a faraway planet with Captain Kirk, Mr. Spock, and Dr. McCoy.

During that first year of our friendship, my parents separated. My family was in turmoil, and as the oldest child, I shouldered the responsibility of being friend, comforter, and confidante to both of my parents. It was a heavy load for a thirteen-year-old. Upon reflection, I now believe that my friendship with Ellen provided an escape from the pressures at home. I immersed myself in a different world with Ellen. Our laughter, fun, and romantic illusions furnished a much-needed release for my turbulent emotions. On the occasions when I talked about my family situation, Ellen listened with compassion and respect. Ellen's friendship was my lifeline.

Like a first love, that first true friendship enveloped me completely. Since that time, I have not been in a friendship with such intensity, with emotions ranging from hilarity to occasional rage to passionate devotion. I adored Ellen.

Many of us spend much of our adult life seeking a friend like this. We read or watch *Anne of Green Gables* and resonate to the friendship of Anne and Diana. As we recall the "bosom friend" of our childhood, we long to experience again the joys of true friendship.

When I spoke about friendship at a retreat recently, Julie approached me with a warm smile. An attractive woman in her late thirties, she exuded vibrancy, enthusiasm, and fun. A few minutes into the conversation, her smile dimmed.

"As you can see, Ann, I'm not a shy or boring person," she began. "But I am desperate for a Christian friend. My husband isn't a Christian, so I can't share many of my deepest thoughts with him. I have been in my church for five years, and I have tried absolutely everything to make friends, but not one person has responded. Everyone seems to have a best friend already. No one has room in her life for me, especially since I'm not part of a 'couple' because my husband doesn't go to church."

I could see the pain in her eyes as she implored, "What am I supposed to do, Ann? I've prayed for five years for a Christian friend. I really need one, and I've done everything I know how to do."

Wherever I go, countless women echo Julie's struggle. We long for something more than the superficial relationships we find at work, in the neighborhood, at church—the "Hi, how are you?" relationships. We long for someone to care about the nitty-gritty details of our lives. We ache for someone to call us up when we're not at church just to say, "I missed you!" We need true friends.

What Is a True Friend?

What exactly is a true friend? One woman gave me this description:

"A true friend is someone who knows what I need without my even asking. Someone who will give me a hug, listen to me, give me a back rub or a compliment. Someone who will watch my kids so I can grocery shop alone, or come over with a bag of bagels and stay for a cup of tea. A friend never sees the mess in my house. Instead, she lends a hand in folding my clothes. She listens without judging but is honest with me when I need straightening out. She never puts down my husband or children but encourages me in loving them. A friend never asks, 'Are you okay?' Instead, she says, 'You seem upset, happy, depressed, etc., today. What can I do for you?'

"I don't have one friend who satisfies all these criteria, but a few come close. My close friends are like oxygen in my life when I feel as if I'm drowning. They are worth more than gold, and I consider them a beautiful gift from God."

Who among us doesn't want a friend like this? We all long for a relationship with someone who understands us completely and is able to meet most, if not all, our relational needs.

Penny, a young woman from Wisconsin, painted an exquisite portrait of true friendship as she shared with me her story:

"My dearest friend Kay has been in and out of my life over the past twenty years since we were in college, but when I truly need her, she was and is always there.

"When my daughter was killed just five years ago, Kay was the first one at my door even though she lived two hours away. She cared for my needs during a time when I was not capable of everyday living because of my grief. She encouraged me to rest, took over my housework, and became the caregiver for my other child during the days between my daughter's accident and the funeral.

"When we returned home from the funeral, Kay and her husband arrived with two pine trees—one for my living daughter and one that would serve as a remembrance for the child I had lost. She and her husband had written a poem for my little daughter about remembering a sister she did not know. It was and still is a cherished gift.

"Just three months after my daughter's death, I suffered a demise pregnancy during my sixteenth week. When it came time for the doctor to induce labor, once again, my friend Kay came to be with me and my husband. She stayed twelve long hours while we waited for the labor to end. We walked the halls, relived college days, and we laughed. Imagine that. During such a painful time. She stayed until I came out of surgery—some twenty hours after she had arrived.

"That was five years ago. We've seen each other only once since then, but we stay in touch, and I know she will be there again . . . when I need her."

Each of us has slightly different expectations of what is meant by *true friendship*. Some use the term *friend* loosely to mean anything from acquaintance to lifelong soul mate. Others are reluctant to call someone a friend because they hold extremely high standards for a friendship. Each friendship is unique because of the two individuals involved.

Yet, as I have reflected on the friendships in my own life, and as I have listened to the stories of hundreds of women across the United States, certain themes recur in varied forms, like the basic themes in a symphony.

Self-Revelation

We long to share ourselves with someone who is eager to hear about our past, our dreams, and the stuff of our daily life. With a true friend, we can be completely honest. We don't need to pretend to be "on top of things," or "together." We can confess our petty jealousies, our struggles, our failures, our sins, knowing that a true friend will not think any less of us. We can also share our successes and victories, knowing she will not become jealous or resentful. She simply accepts us.

When Martha moved in with our family five years ago, we hardly knew each other. We certainly considered her a friend, or we would not have invited her. Yet, despite an arduous two-way interview concerning the proposed living arrangements, all of us were in for some surprises.

The business of living together stripped away the masks of polite friendship and exposed us to one another. We saw each other's strengths and weaknesses. We saw sin and failure as well as righteousness and success. Through all the ups and downs, we remained committed to one another. We were able to reveal ourselves because we knew that the other accepted us and loved us, no matter what.

Martha lived with us for three years, and I consider those three years my graduate course in friendship. Today Martha is one of my closest friends.

Last fall when I was going through a particularly dark and painful time with one of my children, I met Martha for breakfast and shared with her the details. I knew that I didn't need to hold anything back from her. Her love for me and my family and her intimate knowledge of us qualified her as a trustworthy friend. I felt completely safe to disclose these things to her, because I knew she would not respond in a way that would make it difficult for me, nor would she divulge my story to anyone else.

Martha did not cajole or advise me. She listened with great empathy, feeling my pain along with me. After listening for the better part of an hour, she asked me if I wanted any input. When I answered in the affirmative, she shared these wise words:

"Your family needs you to be centered on Christ right now, Ann. Find your strength in him and communicate that strength to the ones who are struggling." Her words carried the ring of truth. They encouraged and refreshed me. Martha was able to help me because we have the kind of friendship in which we can be completely open and honest.

Support

A true friend is someone we look to for support. She is always on our team, cheering us on to victory. When we have a problem, she does not try to solve it for us. Instead, she listens and expresses her solidarity. When our perspective has become distorted by self-pity, she encourages us, not with pat answers but by gently pointing us toward the truth.

There is never a hint of criticism from a true friend. That doesn't mean she doesn't sometimes say hard things. She is the one who asks the tough questions. But we know that her intentions for us are only good. Anyone can say what we want to hear. A true friend tells us what we need to hear. Yet, every word is prompted by love.

Beth and I met for coffee one morning during a period in which I had a very heavy speaking schedule and my family was going through a crisis. I poured out my heart, and Beth listened. When I concluded, Beth asked, "But what about you, Ann? You're taking care of everyone else, but who is taking care of you?"

Later that day, Beth stood at my door with a bulging envelope in her hand. "This is for you to open on the plane tomorrow, Ann," she said.

The next morning as I flew to Grand Rapids, I ripped open Beth's envelope. Out fell a snack-size bag of M&M's (true comfort food!). I unfolded her letter and read words of encouragement. Beth expressed her confidence in me and in God's work in my life, and she enclosed a lovely prayer. I turned toward the window so that my seatmate could not see the tears that slipped down my cheeks as I silently offered up my own prayer of thanks for such a supportive friend.

Service

A true friend shows her love in practical ways. She is someone we can count on to help us out in a pinch. We don't worry about calling on her when a need arises because she always seems to enjoy showering us with deeds of kindness.

A young mother of four told me how her friend Bonnie demonstrated her love in a practical way:

"One morning I woke up with a high fever, chills, aches—the works. I couldn't get out of bed. My husband had important meetings at work. He got the oldest child off to school, and then called Bonnie to see if she could drive our four-year-old to preschool. I didn't know how I would take care of our baby and our two-year-old, and I confess that when my husband left for work, I felt pretty sorry for myself. I lay in bed crying, wishing my mother were here to take care of me like she did when I was a child.

"Bonnie arrived early to pick up Ethan for preschool. She came in and dressed the little ones. She set up a table next to my bed with a pitcher of ice water, a bottle of soda, crackers, orange slices, and some aspirin. She informed me that she was taking my children for the day, and my job was to rest and concentrate on getting better. She asked if she could take my van, since my kids and her kids couldn't all fit in her car.

"That night when Bonnie brought my children home, she also returned a van that sparkled inside and out. Bonnie and the kids had taken the van to the car wash and had vacuumed the inside as well as washing and waxing the exterior. The kids thought it was a great adventure! What a practical act of friendship!"

Our Need for Connection

As wonderful as all this sounds, perhaps friendship is the icing on the cake of life. These days many women are literally running from sunup to sundown to meet their obligations—paying the bills, taking care of their families, or finishing their education. Friendship seems a luxury they cannot afford. Or is it?

Cheryl, Judy, and Christine walk together for exercise early each morning. Cheryl is a small business owner in addition to being a wife and mother. At the beginning of the year, she faced a seemingly impossible business deadline. Financial ruin loomed like a specter. Strain was evident in Cheryl's demeanor. Usually a perennially upbeat and fun-loving person, she was now often close to tears. Judy and Christine listened, encouraged, and tried to provide moral support.

Judy and Christine conferred and decided to offer Cheryl some practical help. They went to work for Cheryl to help her meet her deadline.

The two friends spent many hours with Cheryl over the following six to eight weeks. They worked together, ate lunch together, and continued to walk together as much as Cheryl's hectic schedule allowed. She maintained her walking, despite unrelenting demands in the other arenas of her life. Cheryl realized that the exercise and the supportive friendships were vital to sustaining her energy level, her motivation, and her positive outlook on life.

"I couldn't have done it without the help of my friends," Cheryl said to Judy and Christine after the completion of the project.

For Cheryl, friends are not a luxury. Friendship made the difference between drowning and keeping her head above water.

The wise King Solomon wrote,

> Two are better than one,
>   because they have a good return for their work:
> If one falls down,
>   his friend can help him up.
> But pity the man who falls
>   and has no one to help him up!
> Also, if two lie down together, they will keep warm.
>   But how can one keep warm alone?
>   Ecclesiastes 4:9–11

Consider the fact that we are created in the image of God, who is a relational being. We bear the stamp of his image in that we, too, are relational. Like God our creator, we desire relationships with others. That is a part of our design.

When God said of Adam, "It is not good for the man to be alone" (Gen. 2:18), I believe that this was more than simply a motivation for creating a wife. In a more general sense, God was saying, "I did not create man to be solitary. He needs companionship even as I desire companionship."

Far from being selfish or a sign of weakness, our need for friends is a part of our God-given nature. Friendships are a means by which God fulfills his good purposes in our lives.

True friends encircle us with the support that we need. Without this circle of friendship, we easily fall prey to discouragement, depression, fear, and self-centeredness. When we are functioning as God designed us, our lives knit together in interlocking circles of trust.

The Trust Circle

When my daughter was in sixth grade, her class went on a retreat. Trained camp counselors led the students in group activities that were designed to teach the children how to work cooperatively. One such exercise was called the trust circle.

The ten children in the group formed a tight circle around the counselor. Keeping her body rigid and her arms folded across her chest, the counselor let herself fall toward the circle. The counselor's feet were still in the center of a circle, like the hands of a clock anchored at the center of the dial. The children prevented her from hitting the ground and supported her weight by passing her around the circle. One child could not have supported the counselor. There were always two or three pairs of hands holding her up and moving her along to the next people in the circle.

Our closest circle of friends operates like that trust circle. We all go through times when, crippled by pain or tragedy, we become dead weight in our relationships. We fall.

Who is there to prevent us from hitting the ground? If we have a large number of acquaintances but no true friends, the circle that they form is too far away. They are not close enough to break our fall.

On the other hand, if we have only a few very close friends, they will not be able to provide a tight circle for us. There will be gaps. And two or three people will soon grow weary.

Lorraine, a lovely woman in her thirties, Kleenex in hand, approached me after one of my talks, and I saw pain in her tear-filled eyes.

"I love my husband, Gregg. I really do," she began. "We weren't Christians when we married, so when I came to Christ ten years ago, I began to pray that Gregg would too. I've tried to be a gentle, loving wife to him so that he could see Jesus in me . . . and I think he really does, but he has never made that commitment. We have three precious children, and each of them is a gift from God.

"But the problem is that Gregg is an alcoholic. This has been a deepening struggle for me as I have watched him become more and more dependent on the bottle. His alcoholism has affected his relationship with our children and with me. I can't trust him to drive the kids to their activities. I can't even leave them alone with him anymore. Recently the situation has grown much worse. My pastor has been meeting with the children and me, preparing us for what he calls an 'intervention.'

"The reason I tell you all this is because I wouldn't be standing here if it weren't for my circle of friends. I couldn't have made it this far without their support. They have listened to me, cried with me, held my hand, cared for my children. There have been many times when I didn't think I could live through another day, and suddenly the phone would ring. It would be one of my friends calling to see how I was doing. She would share an encouraging Bible verse or pray with me on the phone. It seems as if God prompts them to call or drop by just when I need to know that he still cares.

"Sometimes I worry that I will wear out these friendships with my neediness. But my friends assure me that they can handle it, and they want to be there for me. What would I have done without them? I don't know what the future holds for our family, but I do have the sense that God is leading me. And his love for me is evident in his provision of this circle of Christian friends."

As she spoke, I envisioned Lorraine standing in the center of a circle of friends. Like the person in the middle of the trust circle, she was dead weight. But as she leaned into the outstretched arms of her friends, there were enough hands to support her. The hands of her friends kept her from falling—their hands supporting her, their hands assisting her, their hands folded in prayer for her.

Finding a True Friend

How does a person find—and keep—true friends like these? That is the subject of the rest of this book.

Yet, in the pursuit of true friendship, I run up against a paradox. When I am full of my neediness, grasping desperately for friendship, I can never find it. My hands always come up empty. The emptier I feel, the harder I grasp, and the more friendship eludes me. Friendship comes, not when I am grasping and needy, but rather when I am full and giving.

There is a place deep within me, the core of my being, that needs to be filled. No human friend can fill this core emptiness. That is a space only Jesus Christ can fill.

Jesus experienced the depth of emotional need, and therefore, he knows our needs and is able to intercede for us as our sympathetic high priest (Heb. 4:15).

In the Garden of Gethsemane, Jesus poignantly revealed his need for true friends and his need for a core relationship with his heavenly Father. Jesus knew what lay ahead for him, namely death on a cross, and he needed time to prepare his heart in prayer. Jesus withdrew with his innermost circle of friends, Peter, James, and John. He implored them to stay awake and pray. His impassioned plea revealed his full humanity and his soul's need for companionship, especially at his darkest hour.

Yet, in Jesus' moment of deepest need, he withdrew a bit farther to be alone with his heavenly Father. In the intimacy of this core relationship, Jesus poured out his heart. The depth of his sorrow, dread, and fear could be known by God alone.

In this intimate glimpse of Jesus found in Matthew 26:36–46, Mark 14:32–42, and Luke 22:39–46, we see that Jesus needed his friends. He wanted them to be near him, supporting him in prayer during his time of soul-wracked anguish.

But his friendships were no substitute for his core relationship with his Father. There was a place in his life so intimate, so deep, so central, where only God could come. In that quiet place, Jesus found the strength, the peace, and the courage to perform the single greatest act of friendship in all of human history. "Greater love has no one than this, that he lay down his life for his friends" (John 15:13).

If you have never opened your heart to the friendship of Jesus Christ, I invite you to do so right now. He waits for you in that quiet place. On the cross, he paid the price for your sin, and he longs to have fellowship with you. All you have to do is open your life to him.

Becoming a True Friend

When I look to Jesus to meet my deepest needs, and I center my life, my goals, my motivations, my dreams, my desires on him, I find greater satisfaction in all my other relationships. This happens because a life centered on Jesus is a life transformed. As I seek him, he changes me little by little, day by day, into someone whose character more and more reflects him. Even my mistakes and failures he uses in this process of transformation.

Jesus, the one True Friend, calls us into friendship with him and into friendship with one another. And he helps us, step by step, to become true friends too. As we find our needs met in him, we have something to give. Slowly our casual friendships characterized by superficiality and self-centeredness are transformed into true friendships that reflect his character.

Questions for Personal Reflection

1. Read Matthew 26:36–46, Mark 14:32–42, and Luke 22:39–46. What strikes you about Jesus' relationships with his friends? His heavenly Father?

2. Read John 15:13. How did Jesus exemplify this kind of friendship? What implications does this have for our relationship with him? With others?

3. In the weeks ahead, what do you hope to learn about true friendship? Write out your thoughts in the form of a prayer.

*A true friend is the greatest
of all blessings, and the one
that we take the least care
of all to acquire.*

La Rochefoucauld

2 For Everything a Season

I surveyed the student lounge and found an empty spot where I could easily observe my fellow students. It was my first morning as a bona fide college student. Because I was living at home and commuting to a university with 40,000 students, I knew that finding friends would take some work on my part. I especially wanted to find Christian friends at this secular institution.

A stocky, blond man (perhaps an upperclassman?) caught my eye. He sat alone at a table with his head bowed, resting his forehead on folded hands. I watched and waited.

Finally, he looked up, and like a vulture, I struck.

"Hi. I'm Ann Martin. I saw you praying, and . . . well, I'm a Christian too," I blurted out.

He blinked and stared at me as if I had just emerged from an alien spacecraft sporting eyeballs on stalks waving from the top of my head.

"I was just resting my eyes," he said in a tone of voice that clearly communicated, "Leave me alone, freshman weirdo." With stammering apologies, I slunk away. So much for the hit-and-miss approach. Too humiliating, I decided.

I turned next to the student newspaper where I investigated the listings of student activities. There it was—Inter-Varsity Christian Fellowship, the Christian group to which my mom had belonged when she had attended the same university thirty years earlier. Several daytime Bible studies were advertised, and I made plans to attend one.

Thus began my search for friendships in my post-Ellen era. My freshman year was one of acute loneliness for me, despite my aggressive approach to making friends. I went on retreats, I asked a fellow freshman (a woman this time) to be my prayer partner, I jumped into leadership in the fledgling commuter group of our InterVarsity chapter—all to no avail. The women I got to know were nice, but nothing really clicked.

Some Enchanted Evening . . .

Perhaps I was waiting for another Ellen—someone whose eyes danced and whose laughter drew me to her with sparkling magnetism.

Occasionally this happens. Our paths cross with someone to whom we are immediately drawn. Eleven years after I first laid eyes on Ellen, I found myself sitting across the living room from someone who cast a similar spell on me. Like Ellen, Debbie's nose crinkled up when she smiled or laughed. She radiated intelligence, humor, and a fun-loving spirit. Once again I said to myself, *We are going to become good friends.*

And we did. Debbie and I have experienced true friendship for sixteen years. We have seen each other through the birth of children and the death of her mother. We have held each other, weeping, during times of pain, and we have laughed until we clutched our sides, gasping for air.

Although it has been many years since we went to the same church, and our lives run in completely different circles now, I have not found it difficult to maintain our friendship. The attraction that drew us together sixteen years ago is just as strong today, and it has been reinforced with commitment and history.

Such friendships are a rarity. Most friendships do not start off with such a strong sense of destiny. If we wait around for someone to whom we feel an overwhelming, irresistible attraction, we may be waiting for the rest of our lives.

Jennifer moved from a major metropolitan area to a relatively small community in North Dakota. Because friendships are very important to Jennifer, she approached her acquaintances at work and church with openness and eagerness. Her initiative paid off and she became friends with a number of women, but the friendships never went beyond a superficial level. Four years later, when her husband was transferred to a different state, Jennifer left without the usual separation pangs. As nice as the women were, Jennifer never connected with any of them.

Jennifer's situation is played out over and over, day after day across America. Women long for a true friend but can't seem to find one.

Take Stock

Unsatisfying though it may be, this season of waiting is a necessary part of the ebb and flow of our lives. The dynamic nature of life in general and friendships in particular guarantees that we will all experience times of loneliness.

Are we simply required to wait? Do we just "gut it out," hoping against hope that a new day will bring the friendship that we so deeply desire?

Absolutely not! Far from being a dry wasteland (although it feels like it is), these seasons of waiting can be the fertile soil from which spring surprising new friendships, new directions for our lives, or deep changes within us.

Times of loneliness are times to take stock of our lives. We only grow through personal reflection, yet most of us spend little time reflecting. When our lives are full and happy, why reflect? We lack any motivation to change, and we're too busy anyway.

When we feel an emptiness, however, like a growling stomach, then we are hungry enough to sit down and consider our options. Loneliness is painful, and pain effectively motivates us to evaluate our situation. For most of us, this is a necessary precursor to growth.

Pray

For the Christian, prayer goes hand in hand with personal reflection. The questions we ask ourselves, as we search our souls, become the questions we ask our heavenly Father. We turn to our comforter and friend to provide for our needs as he has promised.

I hate to admit it, but I usually take a "Why pray when I can do something about it?" approach. I don't really believe that, but you would think so by my actions. When faced with a need, I pick up the telephone or roll up my sleeves rather than dropping to my knees.

Yet, the Bible is replete with incredible promises about prayer. In John 14:13–14, Jesus assured his disciples, "And I will do whatever you ask in my name, so that the Son may bring glory to the Father. You may ask me for anything in my name, and I will do it." In John 16:24, he continued, "Until now you have not asked for anything in my name. Ask and you will receive, and your joy will be complete." James reiterated this message when he said, "You do not have, because you do not ask God" (James 4:2). God delights in giving his children good things. He wants to lavish on us an abundance of blessings. And true friends are among his best gifts. Yet, he waits for us to look to him to supply this need. He does not want us to remain ignorant blessing-consumers. It is in our best interest to know and love the provider of those blessings, so he waits for us to acknowledge him before he bestows on us the gift of true friendship.

When Linda opened her heart to Jesus Christ, her Christian friends numbered zero. Her roommate and her co-workers did not share her beliefs, and their lifestyles were far from a reflection of Christian standards. Linda struggled to follow Christ alone, but she felt as if she was losing ground. She returned to the church of her childhood, but the only people there who were remotely close to her age were a single man who was teaching a Sunday school class for college-age adults, and a young married couple who was assisting him. Linda was the only attendee of the class. Not much friendship potential there!

The married couple invited Linda and Chris, the teacher, over for dinner. That afternoon, Linda reached a point of desperation in her loneliness and her struggle with sin and the pull of her former life.

"Please, God, send me a Christian friend," she begged. That night, as Linda and the wife were clearing the table, the woman turned to her and asked, "Linda, would you like to get together with me once a week to study the Bible and pray, just the two of us?"

Linda's eyes widened and her mouth dropped open. She recognized immediately that this was God's direct answer to her prayer. Her awed, "Yes! Yes, I would!" marked the beginning of a precious friendship that Linda and I have shared for the past eighteen years.

God does not always answer our prayers for a friend with immediacy, however. God's timing is not our timing. We may think we need a friend right now, but God, who knows all things, has a reason for making us wait. So we wait and pray—sometimes for months, sometimes for years.

Jamie wrote to me about persevering in prayer for a true friend:

"I prayed for fifteen years for a special Christian friend. Many times during those fifteen years I became discouraged because God never sent that one special friend. However, I never gave up praying for God to send her to me. Pat came into my life January 26th of this year. We met when we were assigned to the same team of a Christian bowling league. She has since told me that she was so lonely after her recent move to the area and that she had been praying that God would send a new friend to her.

"She, like I, had had many friends but not an intimate best friend. We both had always lived independent lives and had never entirely unmasked ourselves with another woman. We've only known each other for four months, but it seems like we've known each other a lifetime. I have been so compelled to do things for Pat. We share our joys, our sorrows, and our love of Christ. We know God put us together."

Fifteen years is a long time to wait and pray. Yet, how very precious is the gift of God-sent friendship when it follows such a season of prayer.

Be Open to Unexpected Friendships

As we pray, we must consider the possibility that God may send us a friend from an unexpected quarter. God rarely works in our lives according to our designs. The friendship of his choosing may be with a woman to whom we feel no natural attraction. It may involve a considerable amount of venturing forth on our part, or it could be as close as our next-door neighbor.

Sometimes it is someone who is very different from us. Mel told me about a surprising, God-given friendship:

"I'm not even sure how it started, but I became friendly with a woman from church who is not at all the kind of person I would have expected to be friends with. She is outgoing and loving, while I am more reserved. She doesn't get all excited about issues like I do. Even in appearances we are opposites. But I believe God knew I was going to need a friend who was available, as opposed to my other friends who are still working. And when the hard times came, she was there."

Take the Initiative

True friendship rarely arrives on our doorstep wrapped up in a bow. Almost always it requires that we take some initiative. There is no way to get around it. We must overcome our fear, step out of our safety zone, and take a risk.

For the gregarious person, this is not a problem. But for those who are naturally reserved or are gun-shy because of past hurts, this prospect fills them with dread.

You do not have to be as bold as I was on that first day at the university in order to extend the hand of friendship to someone. It can be an easy and natural step in the course of your activities. Sometimes taking initiative means becoming involved in activities where friendships can blossom naturally.

A good example is that of Jamie, who met her best friend, Pat, on a Christian bowling team. She never would have discovered this friend if she had only shown up at church on Sunday. Large gatherings simply do not promote the building of significant personal relationships. Large gatherings are good places to feel lost, intimidated, and isolated. The bowling team had the advantages of being small and very informal. It put people together who shared an interest. And it provided the opportunity for Jamie and Pat to get to know one another almost by accident, while their attention was on bowling. It was a low-pressure, low-risk way to make friends.

Sometimes we are afraid to take the initiative because we feel insecure about having people in our home. We don't feel comfortable entertaining. Our house isn't clean enough. Our cooking isn't gourmet. Our children might misbehave and humiliate us.

I truly understand these feelings. I am sometimes invited to homes that look as if they are straight from the pages of *Better Homes and Gardens.* The hostess takes us on a house tour from top to bottom, even flinging open the closet doors. Everything is spotless and in good taste. *I couldn't get my house that clean if I worked nonstop for a month!* I say to myself. I think about the worn-out carpeting in my living room and dining room with its big, brown stains. I can't compete, so I am tempted to hang back and not invite anyone to my house.

But friendship is not about impressing people. Friendship is about making someone feel loved. And that can happen in a messy, worn-out house as readily as in a lovely one. When I go to a new friend's house and find it looking messy and lived-in, I feel relieved. It puts me at ease—so much so that occasionally I say something I later regret.

My friend Noreene recently reminded me that the first time she invited me into her house, I looked around and said, "I struggle with clutter too." I would not recommend that as an opening line when initiating a friendship. Fortunately, Noreene has a great sense of humor.

Our attempts at initiating friendship will not always meet with success. When Rosemary moved into our neighborhood, I took initiative with a capital *I!* The van had barely pulled up to the house before I was there, carrying boxes. I brought over a meal so that they wouldn't have to cook that night. In the weeks that followed, I invited Rosemary shopping with me, which she seemed to enjoy. I told her where to get the best buys in our area (my specialty). And after they were settled in, we invited Rosemary and her husband over for a dinner party.

Rosemary never reciprocated. "Maybe I came on too strong," I mused to my husband. "Or maybe I said something that offended her." I lapsed into silence as I tried to recall all that I had said in our various encounters. Jim simply shrugged and said, "Forget it, Ann. You've got plenty of other friends. Don't worry about it." After a few more attempts (carefully toned-down attempts), which also met with no response, I finally threw in the towel. But this rejection haunted me.

I will probably never know why Rosemary never returned my offer of friendship. There is an element of mystery involved in friendship as in love, which is why it is such a fascinating and wonderful thing.

Know When to Move On

We need to know when to move on to new arenas if friendship is not happening in our current location, which is what I had to learn with Rosemary.

In chapter one I mentioned Julie, the outgoing, friendly woman who tried for five years to break into the cliques in her church, but to no avail. She prayed, fervently and persistently. She got involved in activities. She volunteered for various ministry opportunities, but no one ever accepted her offers to help. She invited women out for coffee or over to her home. Either they were already busy, or if they came, they never reciprocated.

After five years of fruitless endeavors, Julie feels rejected and alone in her church. In fact, she feels invisible. She realizes that if she stops coming, no one will even notice.

Julie has decided it is time to move on to a different church. She has given her current church a fair shake. She needs to find a church where she can be incorporated into the body, where she can make use of her spiritual gifts for the benefit of others, and where she can receive the blessings of friendship and others' spiritual gifts.

Those of us who are established in churches must never forget what it is like to be brand-new, seemingly the only new person in a group of people who already know each other. It is horribly intimidating. The onus for taking initiative rests not on the newcomer but on those of us who are established.

We don't try to freeze newcomers out of our churches. We so rarely see our friends, however, that when we see them at church, we are dying to catch up with them. Add to that equation the fact that we have responsibilities to discharge (getting our children to Sunday school, teaching children's church, rushing to the choir room), or we try to take care of committee business on the fly on Sunday morning in order to save ourselves a telephone call. Is it any wonder that newcomers are ignored? And it's true: We sometimes don't miss them. They quietly slip out the back door and never return.

We need to be reminded constantly that we should take care of business and nurture our friendships outside of Sunday mornings or other times when newcomers may be present. Our efficiency-mindedness will be the death of us. We must think less about saving ourselves time and effort. And we surely must think less about doing what is comfortable for ourselves. Reaching out to newcomers is a matter of simple obedience to Jesus Christ. That is what Jesus would do.

If you are in Julie's situation, do not entertain any guilt about leaving the church, group, or club to which you belong. If you have had a positive approach and have done everything you can to take initiative for a reasonable amount of time, but still to no avail, go ahead and try another group. There are plenty of churches and other organizations that desperately need you.

Reevaluate

If, on the other hand, you find yourself floating from group to group, church to church, never finding friendships, always encountering rejection, perhaps the problem is not the groups or the churches. Perhaps the problem is you.

One woman told me this story:

"Many years ago I was on the board of a community organization. One woman, Trisha, a fellow board member, complained that she had been involved in the organization for several years, but no one had reached out to her in friendship. As we served together on the board over the following year, I began to see why. Trisha had a control problem. She tried to tell everyone how to do their jobs. When they didn't do things the way she dictated, she made sarcastic remarks behind their backs. She gave them dirty looks. In short, she could be mean. The natural consequence of her behavior was that people learned to keep their distance."

Chances are you are not a mean, nasty person. But perhaps you have some blind spots in the way you relate to people. Perhaps the way you voice your opinion shuts other people down. Perhaps you give your friends advice when what they really want is a listening ear. Perhaps you appear

so perfect and together that others feel inadequate around you. Or perhaps you are so needy that friendship with you requires more than anyone less than Mother Teresa is willing to give.

The time has come to examine your life. What changes can you make so that others will desire and seek your friendship? The following chapters explore these and many other issues that arise in friendship. Take heart. We all have blind spots. We all are sinners, and except for Jesus, we can only take sinners as friends. That is the starting point.

It is not the last word, however. The last word is Jesus. If we have given our lives to him, he is at work within us to change us and to make us more like him. As we explore the many facets of true friendship, let us open our hearts to his transforming power. We must face our mistakes and our inadequacies in order to learn the lessons he has for us. Only then can we move toward becoming a true friend and experiencing the fullness of true friendship.

Questions
for Personal
Reflection

1. Can you recall extended periods of time when you
   have had to wait for a true friendship? Describe
   your thoughts and feelings during that time.

2. Jesus said to his disciples, "You did not choose
   me, but I chose you and appointed you to go and
   bear fruit—fruit that will last" (John 15:16).
   What does this tell us about Jesus' approach to
   friendship?

3. Do you think it is important to examine yourself
   and your relationships? Why or why not?

*One friend in a lifetime is
much; two are many; three
are hardly possible.*

Henry Adams

3 *The Balancing Act*

*D*ebbie and I settled in with our cups of steaming coffee for our forty-five-minute oasis of conversation. We rendezvous at the bookstore's espresso bar once every couple of weeks while her older son is having his piano lesson. Our different lifestyles work against our spending time together: Debbie homeschools her two sons, and I am often writing or traveling for speaking engagements. We consider these espresso bar moments a major triumph for our friendship.

Today Debbie began, "Ann, I need to ask you a question. Have I offended you in any way?"

"Of course not, Debbie! What have I done that gave you that idea?" I asked.

"You just haven't been calling me. That's just not like you, not to be in touch."

I reflected over the past six weeks. It was true. I had picked up the phone to call my dear friend only once or twice. The reason was not hurt feelings but a busy schedule. I found I couldn't maintain everything, and the first thing to go was my time on the telephone keeping in touch with my closest friends.

Relieved that she was not at fault, Debbie understood my reasons, forgave my neglect, and we moved on to our next topic of conversation. Yet, I was saddened that in my flurry of activity, I had disregarded one of my most precious treasures—my true friend.

Time is an essential ingredient in cultivating true friendship. If we do not spend time with a friend, that friendship is likely to wither and die like a neglected houseplant. And if we are not available when our friend needs us, we communicate that we do not really care about her. A true friend takes time for friendship, especially when she is needed.

Brenda, a young mother of two preschoolers, related the following tale when I spoke at her church in Minnesota:

"Not too long ago, I slipped on the ice and was afraid that I had injured my knee. I called my friend Zoe and asked her if she could give me a ride to the doctor. 'I'm just on my way to exercise class, Brenda,' she said. 'I'll drive you after class.'"

To Zoe's credit, she later realized that she had been less than a true friend to Brenda. She telephoned Brenda and apologized for being so caught up in her own schedule that she had let her down.

I would like to think I would never do something like that, yet I know my agenda has interfered with my ability to be a true friend on more than a few occasions.

That Was Then, This Is Now

When my mother was raising my sisters and me back in the 50s and 60s, she was at home during the day, as were all the other mothers in the neighborhood. Nearly every afternoon about an hour before the children arrived home from school, a group of moms met for coffee. They shared their struggles and their triumphs with an Erma Bombeck attitude. They helped each other see the humor in the daily ups and downs of family life.

It was more than fun and games, however. Those friends supported each other through marital difficulties, divorce, erring children, accidents, cancer, death. When our next-door neighbor Louise revealed that the doctors had discovered she had cancer, a shock wave rippled through the neighborhood. The entire "Deer Hill gang" rallied. The women brought casseroles, visited Louise at home and in the hospital, and provided support through her treatment, decline, and death.

Thirty years later, most of the women no longer live in Deer Hill, but many of the friendships remain strong. Recently, Camille lost her husband of forty-plus years in a sudden heart attack. Peggy, one of the friends who still lives in the neighborhood, saw the ambulance and investigated. She got on the telephone and alerted the other Deer Hill friends. The next day, my mom stopped by, casserole in hand, to show her love and support for her former neighbor and true friend. The bonds between these friends are strong. They were forged by time—many hours spent together over many years.

Life is not as simple now as it was back in the 50s and 60s. Most women work outside the home either full- or part-time. Many who stay at home choose to educate their children at home as well, so they become full-time educators in addition to all their other roles. We want our children to have every advantage so they will grow up to be productive, successful adults; hence, we fill their "free" moments with extracurricular, enriching activities. That means when we are not working or seeing to the basics of food, clothing, and shelter, we are driving children to soccer practice, piano lessons, karate . . . the list goes on. Many single Christian women log in long hours at the workplace, then grab dinner on the way to an evening church committee meeting, Bible study, or volunteer activity. They finally arrive at home in time to collapse into bed, only to repeat the drill the following day.

We long for a simpler lifestyle, yet, truth be told, we don't want to go back to the 50s. We fancy ourselves smarter, more independent than our mothers were. But something is missing. We find ourselves more isolated than our mothers were, and one reason for this seems obvious: We no longer have time to chat over coffee with a group of friends, let alone develop deep and satisfying friendships. Instead, we often maintain friendships on the run. But being friendships of convenience, they come and go as our lives slip in and out of various spheres of activity.

One woman told me, "Busyness is one of the biggest barriers of all time to friendship. The pace of my life is sometimes overwhelming, yet I know I am not nearly as busy as so many I observe. . . . I yearn to be a good friend, but I am painfully aware of my own busyness and distractions and selfish ways. There is a neighbor in my block who is in great need of friendship. She is brand-new to the area, a new mother. The combination is dreadfully stressful to her, I'm sure. I took her out to lunch with several neighborhood women to introduce her around. I have stopped in to see her and actually went to a bingo night with her. I enjoy being with her, but when I get busy at home, she sometimes stops by to visit and I just can't. I pray that I can be flexible and available and loving to those clearly in need."

Is there a way to enjoy deeper friendships without neglecting our chores, quitting our jobs, or giving up home-schooling? Or are there times in our lives when friendships simply are not practical?

Friendship and the Seasons of Life

Kathy A. and I have been friends for twelve years. We met in a women's Bible study when our children were young. Our sons went to preschool together. Often, after Bible study, we ended up at one or the other's house, eating sandwiches and chatting while our children played together. It was difficult to follow the thread of continuity in our conversations, for we were interrupted every few minutes by some childish eruption. How we longed for the day when our children would be in school and we could get together and actually complete a sentence!

The day finally arrived when all our children were in school, but instead of being freer, our lives seemed to get busier. I became involved with women's ministry, writing books and speaking, and Kathy enrolled in graduate school. Now that our children were older, their activities also dictated our schedules. Our get-togethers dwindled from several times a week to several times a year. We laugh now about how bogged down we thought we were during those preschool years, yet how very ripe those years were for friendship.

Different seasons of our lives present us with differing degrees of availability for friendship. Generally, the fewer responsibilities we have, the greater our availability for friendship. Children are a huge responsibility, and nurturing and training them requires an overwhelming amount of a mother's time. For this reason, the single woman without children and the empty nester may have more time to pursue friendship than do the homeschooling mother of four and the single mom who holds down a full-time job.

We need not feel guilty if our present life situation affords us little time for the "let's do lunch" type of friendship. Perhaps this is a season for developing friendships with our husband or our children. Or perhaps we need to explore new, more creative ways to spend time with friends.

If we belong to Jesus Christ, the Bible assures us that all our circumstances are a part of our Father's loving, sovereign plan (Rom. 8:28). The fact that I am a wife and mother is neither an accident nor is it entirely of my doing. God called me to this place. He has given me a job to do, namely, to love my family. This takes a significant amount of my time and energy right now. Instead of wishing these years away, I need to focus on being the wife, mother, and friend that God would have me be right now, within the parameters of my responsibilities.

Maximizing Time with Friends

We all have duties to perform in the normal course of our lives. These are the things that seem to mitigate against time with friends. One way to spend time with friends is to invite them to join us in these endeavors. And, of course, we can make friends with women who are doing the same activities we are doing. That way, we are not "taking time out" for friendship. Our time with friends happens in conjunction with the fulfillment of our other obligations. Here are some suggestions:

Friendship and Exercise

Between Arlington to the east and Purcellville to the west and north, the Washington & Old Dominion Trail winds its way through forty-eight miles of northern Virginia. This trail runs directly behind my house and provides year-round entertainment as we watch from our windows the continual procession of people and pets.

Several years ago I had a brilliant inspiration. Here was a means of exercise literally at my doorstep for which I needed no membership and no expensive equipment. I could avail myself of it at any time of the day. I donned my tennis shoes and headed out the back door, and thus, I became a walker.

For a half hour to forty-five minutes, I traversed the path in relative solitude each day that my schedule and the weather permitted. I treasured these moments of prayer and reflection. The walks energized me not only physically but spiritually and emotionally as well.

Before long, I came to recognize all the other "regulars" who walked my early morning hour. Among them was a curious group—an older man and two "younger" women ("younger" being approximately my age!). I thought of them as "the man and his harem." After greeting one another for many weeks, we finally introduced ourselves. I met J. P., a retired gentleman, and Noreene and Sandy, the younger women. They were so warm and friendly that when they invited me to join their walking group, I took them up on their offer.

So began our friendship. It sprang not out of mutual attraction or shared values but out of our desire for exercise and schedules that happened to jibe. Yet, in the process of walking together, we began to share who we are with one another. Almost before we realized what was happening, we found ourselves caring for each other. Our commitment to one another crossed over the boundary of the bike path, spilling into other areas of our lives. We learned that we could count on the others. We have become true friends.

Like my mother and her dear friends from the neighborhood, my walking group and I see each other every day. We, too, share our daily joys and sorrows. We talk about everything from child-rearing issues to books and music to dinner menus to professional concerns. We cheer each other on through good times and bad. Yet, all this takes place while we are getting our exercise!

Do you already spend time exercising? Why not invite a friend to join you? Do you need to spend time exercising? (If you answered no to the first question, then the answer to this question is yes!) Exercise with a friend. The conversation keeps your mind off the discomfort or drudgery of exercise. Soon you will find yourself looking forward to your exercise time because you enjoy spending time with your friend.

Friendship and Work

For those with jobs outside the home, work is a natural place to begin to develop friendships. Here is what Marci, a young, single career woman says:

"I've made a lot of terrific friendships at work. There are two different kinds of work friendships: the ones that are just friends at work and the ones that develop into all-encompassing friendships. The first kind can still be very close friends, because you have so much in common. They're in the fray with you all the time. They know all the stresses, all the personalities. When you are spending eight to ten hours a day thinking about work, these friends share a good portion of your life. You hang around at work together, go out to lunch, travel together, and generally have a great time.

"When I want to see if a work friendship might develop into an all-encompassing friendship, I test it out. I invite the friend to do something outside the work environment. We go out to dinner or take in a movie and have coffee afterward. We sit and talk and share our interests. If we find that we have enough in common outside of work to pursue a friendship, then we begin to do things regularly after hours.

"One of my close friendships began as a work friendship and developed into an all-encompassing one. My friend and I share everything with one another. I know more about her than the rest of her friends do because we have work in common in addition to everything else—and that's such a huge part of both of our lives."

If you work outside the home, perhaps you can develop your friendships with coworkers through utilizing snippets of time here and there. Usually it is not a matter of time but of attitude. A smile and a kind word can open the door to friendship, and they take no time at all.

Perhaps your job is raising your children or homeschooling. There are many other busy but lonely mothers out there. Seek out others in your same situation. See if there are some jobs you can do together. Going to the shopping mall and the playground count as work. These activities definitely improve with the company of a friend.

Debbie and I cherish our early memory of baking thumbprint cookies together one December. I misread the recipe and put in one pound of butter instead of one cup. The first batch ran in puddles on the cookie sheet when baked. Then, in trying to correct my error, I added too much flour. To rectify this, I had to add still more butter. In the end, we baked eight times the orginal recipe. We had more thumbprint cookies than you can shake a stick at, and we laughed until the tears ran down our cheeks. In this particular case, our camaraderie did not make the work any easier (I may not have made those errors if working alone), but it sure was a lot more fun. And I discovered a true friend in the process.

Friendship and Hobbies

Many of us find time to pursue a hobby or leisure activity. Like exercise and work, hobbies provide natural opportunities to develop friendships. Shared interests form an unforced basis for friendship.

Some hobbies lend themselves to friendship more readily than others. Needlework is a perfect example. Eight years ago, several women from my church decided to get together one evening a week to work on their individual needlework projects. They call themselves the Stitch 'n Pray group. Four to six women gather weekly to gab, do cross-stitch, needlepoint, even household mending, and share prayer requests. They decided not to make it a heavy-duty prayer time but a relaxed time of socializing.

La Verne, one of the four charter members of the group, related to me how friendships have grown from this shared activity:

"Several of these women are now my best friends. If something is going on in my life and I need prayer, I just call them up and leave a message on their answering machine. We don't see each other exclusively on Wednesday nights. We talk frequently throughout the week. It took a long time to get beyond the superficial and really become intimate friends, but in the past several years, that is what has happened. We've seen each other through a lot."

Even if your hobby is a solitary one such as reading, you can turn it into a friendship-deepening pursuit. Form a book club. Or simply pass your book on to a friend; then discuss it together over the telephone or over a cup of tea.

Hiking, tennis, biking, music (performance or listening), movies, shopping—the list is endless. Just about anything you enjoy doing can be done with a friend.

Tracy works full-time and has two elementary school-age children to care for when she gets home from work, so our get-togethers have grown infrequent. Among other things, Tracy and I share a love of good food (Tracy subscribes to *Gourmet* magazine). When either of us travels on business, we call each other up and recount the details of the culinary delights we enjoyed on our trip. Sometimes when I am in the middle of preparing a recipe and need to make a substitution, I call Tracy. She serves as my cooking consultant. So even eating and cooking are hobbies that can be shared with a friend!

Friendship and Ministry

People call me the Thrift Shop Queen. I'm always bragging about my fabulous new outfit for under ten dollars. Because I love to shop at thrift shops, my ears perked up when the women who run our church's thrift shop put out a plea for volunteers. When it came time to sign up for a specific time slot, I scrutinized the list of volunteers. I saw the name of an acquaintance from our women's ministry, a woman named Jackie whom I wanted to get to know better. I called Jackie and asked if she would like to work at the thrift shop with me. For one year, Jackie and I spent four hours a month volunteering in the thrift shop together. We talked as we worked, and over the months we built a friendship.

If you are involved in a church, you probably are involved in serving. Whether it be hospital visitation, teaching Sunday school, preparing meals for the homeless, or serving on a committee, the joy of serving God is magnified when it is shared with a friend. Recruit a friend to join you in your task—or make friends along the way.

Friendship and Prayer

I know of no better way to deepen a friendship than to join with a friend in prayer on a regular basis.

Juanita, from California, told me about her prayer partnership:

"About five years ago in the fall, I was acutely lonely. I recognized that I had lots of acquaintances and surface relationships, but no one besides my husband who knew, day to day, what was happening with me. I tend to be a giver, and a listener—a good listener—but enough of an introvert that I don't easily open up or express my own needs.

"At that low point, I asked the Lord to give me a friend and to teach me interdependency, rather than my usual self-sufficiency. And then a woman whom I didn't know well asked me to be her prayer partner. We were so different. She was single—divorced—without children, a working woman, with a load of pain and insecurity. I had a family, children in their teens, and I was a homemaker and a leader at church.

"Despite these differences, we have met every week for an hour for the past five years. We talk about our lives, different as they are, and our needs or joys, and we pray for each other. It has to be early in the morning, but neither of us would miss it for the world.

"I've seen my friend grow in confidence and healing of her pain. Now she's a wonderful leader. And God has taken my loneliness away. I have learned to be a receiver as well as a giver. It's been a gift from my loving Lord."

If you have never had a prayer partner, please take a risk and invite someone to embark on this adventure for a specified period of time. It's easier to make an initial commitment when it has a beginning and an end. That way, if the chemistry doesn't work, you can graciously part ways at the end.

Not all prayer partnerships become true friendships. But often they do. And we all need to pray more and have the prayer support of others. Amazing things happen when we join with a friend in prayer.

Focus on a Few

No matter how creative and efficient we are in combining friendship with our other responsibilities, we still face time limitations. I struggle with this constantly. Friendships are like material possessions: The longer we live in one place, the more we accumulate. After living in the Washington, D.C., area for eighteen years, I have accumulated many wonderful friendships. And I want to be a good friend to all these special women in my life (I want to be the best of friends, if the truth be known). Yet, that takes time, more time than I can devote to all these friendships.

Sylvia has a similar dilemma. She approaches it this way:

"You need to write on your calendar to remember to call friends or drop by if you're like me—independent and pretty happy to go long stretches without contact. That tendency of mine is not conducive to friendship, so I must make an effort.

"Some of my friendships are more important to me than others. I try to get in touch or get together with each person based on my level of commitment. This sounds cold, but it is practical with all the competing demands in my life."

When I feel frustrated by time limitations and overwhelming demands, I take comfort in the example of Jesus. People and responsibilities pulled at him from every direction. Unlike me, Jesus truly had the wisdom and the power to help all those people. Yet, he didn't. He didn't heal everyone. He wasn't best friends with everyone. Jesus listened carefully to the heavenly Father then did the job he was given to do.

Jesus chose twelve with whom he would share his life, and of those twelve, he chose three to be his closest friends. Even Jesus' time was limited. He could not be all things to all people. He focused on a few.

If we find that we are spread too thin, we should ask God to show us the friendships on which he would have us focus. Better to go deep with a few than to have superficial relationships with many. The bottom line is, in order to have friends, we must be a friend—and being a friend takes time.

When people hear that I walk six to eight miles each day, they invariably ask, "How do you have the time?" My reply: "I don't have the time. I just do it." True, other things don't get done. (Housecleaning comes to mind.) But for various reasons, I have decided that walking is a priority for me. So I spend time walking.

Similarly, if true friendship is our priority, we will somehow make time to develop our friendships. We will be there for our friends when they need us. Possessions, programs, accomplishments—all these things will pass away. People are eternal. When we spend time giving ourselves in love to other people, we invest in something of eternal worth. Becoming a true friend means giving ourselves—and our time—to someone, and in so doing, demonstrating the sacrificial, others-focused love of Jesus Christ.

Questions for Personal Reflection

1. What is it about your season of life that makes it difficult (or easy) to find time for friends? How does Romans 8:28 apply to your situation?

2. What activities in your life could you creatively combine with friendship? (Think about activities such as exercise, work, hobbies, ministry, prayer . . .)

3. Look at Mark 9:2–8 and John 21:15–22. Reflect on Jesus' example of focusing on a few. How might you apply this principle to your friendships?

*Oh, the comfort, the inexpressible
comfort of feeling safe with a person:
having neither to weigh thoughts nor
measure words, but to pour them out.
Just as they are—chaff and grain
together, knowing that a faithful hand
will take and sift them, keep what is
worth keeping, and then with the
breath of kindness, blow the rest away.*

George Eliot

4 A Safe Haven

*L*iz sat in the booth waiting for Tina. As the minutes ticked by and Tina didn't come, Liz began to reflect over the past two years of her life. It was not a pretty picture.

Today was her birthday, a stark reminder of her still-single status. In the two years since her fortieth birthday, her parents had both died, leaving her feeling orphaned. Sometimes the pain was almost unbearable. Married friends just didn't understand what it was like for a single person to lose both parents. She felt like a small boat adrift in a vast and turbulent sea. She longed for the mooring of marriage, but at her age, with no prospects in the picture, the chances seemed rather remote. There had been someone . . . Liz had cherished high hopes for her relationship with Rick. Just when it looked like things might move toward marriage, everything seemed to unravel. Four weeks ago, Rick had broken off their relationship. Liz was still reeling from shock and pain. Now, on top of these losses, Liz's job was in jeopardy. She didn't know how much more pain and uncertainty she could stand.

Tina slid into the booth across from Liz and wished her happy birthday. They hadn't seen each other in several months, so they had a lot of catching up to do. Liz began to pour forth her woes, certain that Tina, who was also single and had lost a parent, would sympathize.

Nothing could have prepared her for Tina's response.

"You know, Liz, I am really tired of listening to all your problems. With you, everything is a crisis. You need to take a more positive approach to life. It's not all doom and gloom, and it certainly isn't very pleasant for your friends to hear nothing but sob stories. We all have problems. Get a grip on your life and make the best of it."

The waiter set their dinners on the table. Liz stared at her food, unable to speak, unable to eat. She felt as if she had been barely standing, bruised and broken, and instead of being received and supported by loving arms, Tina had bowled her over with a wrecker's ball. Liz has no recollection of the remainder of their evening together. She managed to stagger to her car, drive home, and crumple into a ball on her bed. Never again would she confide in Tina. Tina's insensitivity to Liz at her most vulnerable moment dealt their friendship a deadly blow.

"I know I can be pretty negative sometimes," Liz admitted to me, "but can I help it that I have had a string of terrible things happen to me? I didn't ask for my parents to die. Maybe I had something to do with Rick ditching our relationship, but it's still painful. I thought Tina would understand. When she went through painful things in the past couple of years, she cried on my shoulder and I tried to be very empathetic.

"What really gets me is that I keep wondering how long she's been harboring these feelings. It must have been building up for a long time and for some reason just erupted that night.

"It wouldn't be so bad if she called to apologize afterward or in some way acknowledged that she had been out of line. But instead she has been cold and distant.

"To tell the truth, at this point, I'd be afraid to say anything of a personal nature to her. I sure don't want to ask to be lined up against the wall and shot all over again."

Liz no longer feels safe in her relationship with Tina. She can't trust Tina to respond to her in a loving manner. She no longer believes that Tina is committed to cheering her on through the good times and the bad.

A true friend provides a safe haven. She accepts us, failures, foibles, and all. She does not judge us when we show her who we are. She responds with gentleness and empathy. She is genuinely on our team. She would never betray us through gossip or by breaking a confidence.

We all expect this from a true friend. But am I that kind of friend? Are you? If we want trustworthy friends, we need to be a trustworthy friend. We must embrace the attitudes and behaviors that will create an environment of safety crucial to true friendship, and we must avoid behaviors that act as safety hazards.

What Makes a Friendship Safe?

Gentleness

Gentleness of manner and attitude paves the way to safety in a friendship. Conversely, if someone reacts to us in an abrupt, harsh, or abrasive manner, we recoil. This hurts us when it comes from anyone, but it especially stings when the wounds are inflicted by someone who is close to us.

Tina's observations may have contained a kernel of truth. Liz might benefit greatly from a more positive approach to life. Yet, Tina's delivery was anything but gentle. Her insensitivity wounded Liz and rendered their relationship unsafe for Liz.

The quality of gentleness comes up frequently in the Bible, often in descriptions of the renewed character of the Christian. Paul wrote in Colossians 3:12, "Therefore, as God's chosen people, holy and dearly loved, clothe yourselves with compassion, kindness, humility, gentleness and patience."

My walking buddy J. P. is a retired Navy man. He told me the story of a sailor on his ship who was always dirty. This young man had never been taught personal hygiene, and his deficiency was evident to his bunk mates. Finally, a group of sailors decided they had had enough. They grabbed him, stripped him, dragged him to the showers, and went at him with hard-bristled scrub brushes. "That's what you call 'peer pressure,'" J. P. joked.

All too often we see the "dirt" on others and we apply the hard-bristled scrub brush. Usually the net effect of this approach is not a cleaner and reformed person but rather a wounded person, scraped and bleeding.

A gentle person tries not to hurt her friend. She does not typically wield a hard-bristled scrub brush—although she will when necessary and when it's in her friend's best interest. She delights in soothing, soft cloths with warm water and fragrant soaps. In other words, when a true friend has something hard to say, she says it with love and kindness so that the sting is removed. She provides loving guidance, not insensitive sandblasts.

We feel safe with such a friend because we know we can trust her not to hurt us unnecessarily. We know her heart desires only good for us. Beyond her intentions, her manner is one that will not send us for a loop. We need never fear that she will use harsh words or looks to wound us. She would never belittle us or betray us because she loves us so deeply.

A gentle person also does not condemn. Although she has her own opinions, and she may not agree with us, we never get the feeling that she is finding fault with us. She does not give us the feeling that she is judging us. Instead, she communicates unconditional acceptance by her manner, her words, and her actions.

Confidence that we are accepted just as we are is liberating. We are strengthened to reach beyond our current limitations by the assurance of continued acceptance. We know that it is okay to try for something and risk failure because our friend accepts us completely, even with our current failures. Through her gentle, noncondemning attitude, a true friend creates a safe place where we can grow.

A gentle person is sensitive to the effects of her words. While she is honest in what she says, she does not necessarily say anything and everything that comes to mind. She weighs her words and considers how they will make her friend feel. She does not simply react in a visceral manner and let the chips (or friends) fall where they may.

Frequently, those of us with strong, outgoing personalities can become strident, especially when our buttons are pushed. We react to a friend's words in a dogmatic or overly emphatic way that shuts her down. She isn't prepared for such a loud blast. She no longer feels safe to offer her observations or opinions.

When I called my friend Lucy recently to set a time when we could get together, she launched into a litany of all her various pressures. After being bombarded by this barrage for several minutes, I was sorry I had suggested getting together. I felt guilty for placing yet another burden on her. I thought an invitation to lunch was a fairly safe thing, but apparently at the time it was not.

Yet, truth be known, Lucy was the one who was feeling guilty. She wanted to spend time with me but felt that she couldn't without neglecting her other responsibilities. She felt guilty she had not been in touch with me. Her bomb blast of woes was simply a manifestation of her own frustration. Nonetheless, her approach was harsh, not gentle.

I know I do the very same thing when someone says something that makes me feel guilty or defensive. I find it very difficult to overcome my "hot button" reactions. But I must if I want my friends and loved ones to feel safe with me, secure that I am "on their team."

We can strive for gentleness, however, without sacrificing honesty. A safe friendship is one where the truth is spoken in love (Eph. 4:15). The manner is always gentle, and the matter is always genuine.

Authenticity

Marie is a pastor's wife and mother of five. When her family first arrived at their new church, Marie was approached by Carrie, young in years but mature in faith and wisdom. Carrie said to her, "You need a friend. You need someone with whom you can be completely honest." Carrie became that friend to Marie. Many of the women in the church would not have been able to handle hearing about the struggles of the pastor's wife (nor would it be appropriate for Marie to share many details of her family life). With Carrie, however, Marie knew she could be completely herself. Why? Because Carrie accepted her. Carrie always responded with gentleness, never judgment or criticism.

Marie's authenticity in turn has set Carrie free to be authentic in their friendship. Carrie told me, "Marie is real. She doesn't put on airs or try to be someone she isn't. Just in being who she is, she makes me feel accepted for who I am. She doesn't hide behind a spiritual mask, yet I know that the desire of her heart is that her relationship with the Lord permeate her life, her heart, her home. She is truthful about herself, thus eliminating any fears that she is trying to be something different for the sake of securing my friendship."

In contrast, Carrie told of another friend with whom she meets on a regular basis for Bible study and prayer:

"I know she is not telling me what she really thinks and feels because she keeps looking for my approval. If I don't say something in agreement immediately, she modifies what she just said. I know she is trying to please me, and it makes me really sad. How can I be her friend when I don't know who she really is?"

Authenticity is both a cause and a result of safety in a friendship. On the one hand, we cannot feel safe in a relationship when we cannot trust the other person to be honest with us about who she is. Phoniness never promotes true friendship. Authenticity provides a basis for safety. On the other hand, most of us cannot be completely honest about who we are until we feel safe in a relationship. Here authenticity is the end result of a safe friendship. Safety is the fertile soil in which authenticity can take root and grow.

What exactly is authenticity in a friendship? In Marie and Carrie's friendship, authenticity meant transparency. There were no pretenses in their friendship. "What you see is what you get." This eliminates guesswork. When we know our friend is the genuine article, we can accept her for who she is and move on from there.

However, if we sense that she is not who she presents herself to be, the friendship does not have a solid foundation. Interactions are built on a mirage. When Carrie observed that her Bible study partner was not sharing her true self, it made Carrie uncomfortable. Carrie continues to be honest, authentic, and transparent for her part, but she finds it much more difficult in this setting because there is a barrier between them.

Authenticity breaks down barriers. When I am with someone who shares with me her struggles and failures, I feel free to do the same. I think, *Oh, good! She's experienced the same feelings I have. She will understand!* On the other hand, when I am with someone who paints a perfect picture of herself, I do not feel safe to reveal my weaknesses. I know I don't live up to those perfect standards.

When the seed of our honest self-revelation finds itself surrounded by the fertile soil of gentleness and understanding, it sends forth a shoot of trust. In this environment of safety, our trust in our friend blossoms and produces more seeds of authenticity. Safety comes from the confidence that we can be ourself with a friend, even as she is completely herself with us, because in the friendship we find mutual acceptance and love.

Empathy

Besides gentleness and authenticity, empathy also contributes to safety in friendships. We feel safe with a friend whom we know will hurt when we experience pain and soar when we experience triumph.

Audrey came home one day to find that her husband had moved out. His personal belongings were gone. All that remained was a note telling her he didn't love her anymore. After fifteen years of marriage and four children, he wanted his freedom. Although Audrey knew their marriage was in trouble, and she suspected that Hank had fallen in love with someone else, she was devastated. This was the last thing in the world she wanted for her life. She felt as if she couldn't go on living.

Darlene, an acquaintance from church, learned that something terrible had happened. She called Audrey, who related the basic facts. Audrey hung up the phone and began to go through the motions of her morning routine. In a daze, she dressed and put breakfast on the table. She was surprised to hear a knock at the door. There stood Darlene, holding a pan of hot, homemade sweet rolls. Darlene set the rolls down in the kitchen and turned to Audrey. Without a word, she encompassed her in a warm embrace. Both women wept for some time. Then in silence, Darlene left.

"In all my life, I have never experienced a greater act of love," Audrey told me. Sweet rolls, a hug, and tears. No advice, no platitudes, no questions, no words at all.

"It would have been so easy for her to come in and start to ask me questions. Lots of other people did in the weeks and months that followed. They wanted to figure out how this could have happened, how it could have been prevented. When the others questioned me, it was horrible. I felt like everyone was scrutinizing my life and judging me, when this was the last thing I ever wanted to happen.

"But Darlene didn't ask me any questions. Her silent embrace and her tears brought me so much comfort."

Darlene demonstrated what Paul meant when he told Christians to mourn with those who mourn (Rom. 12:15). We feel safe in a friendship when we know that our friend is not judging us. In our moment of pain, she is not trying to figure it out, place blame, or fix the problem. She is simply weeping.

The same verse instructs us to rejoice with those who rejoice. This is the other side of empathy. We see an excellent example of this in Psalm 20: "May the LORD answer you when you are in distress; may the name of the God of Jacob protect you. . . . May he give you the desire of your heart and make all your plans succeed. We will shout for joy when you are victorious and will lift up our banners in the name of our God. May the LORD grant all your requests" (vv. 1, 4–5).

The writer voices his solidarity with the one to whom he writes when he says, "We will shout for joy when you are victorious." That is positive empathy!

It seems as though rejoicing should be easier, but often it is harder to rejoice with our friends than to weep with them. We can readily identify with our friends when they share pain and failure. These experiences are universal. But our successes separate us from one another. When a friend

bubbles over with joy about a personal victory, we think,
I could never do that, or *That will never happen to me.*
This brings us to the first safety hazard.

Safety Hazards

Jealousy

Competition and jealousy rob us of our ability to delight
freely in a friend's triumphs. Insecure creatures that we
are, we turn our focus back on ourselves instead of losing
ourselves in our friendship. We have such glaring needs to
be seen as competent, lovable, and successful that we are
constantly evaluating who we are in light of those around
us. Others' successes become a measuring stick with which
we measure our own worth.

If we can simply grab hold of the fact that God loves us
completely, however, failures, foibles, and all, then we are
on the road to understanding that we don't need to prove
ourselves. Therein lies the key to a true friendship, where
our focus can be entirely on our friend and not on ourselves.

Rita and I became friends the moment we met. We had
so much in common. We were involved in the same activities, our children were the same ages, and our gifts lay in
the same areas. Competition first cropped up with respect
to our children. Her children walked sooner, talked more
proficiently, socialized better, and learned more quickly.
Then we found ourselves vying for the same positions in
various organizations. Once again I felt outshone by my
friend. She was attractive and articulate as well as my intel-
lectual superior.

Did I rejoice in her successes? No. I began to look for
flaws in her perfection. *If only she weren't so perfect, I
wouldn't feel so inadequate,* I thought. Then when I noticed a chink in her armor, I didn't keep it to myself. When
Rita's name came up in conversation (and often I was the

one to bring it up), I passed along my observation. She isn't as perfect as she seems, I communicated. These attitudes and behaviors erected a barrier between Rita and me.

The turning point came for me when I finally acknowledged my sin. I confessed my sin to a trusted prayer partner. As she prayed for me, I realized that my sin was not only against Rita. I was sinning against God. My jealousy said to God, "I am not content with the way you made me. And I'm not crazy about the circumstances that you have brought into my life either. If you just gave me the advantages you have given Rita, everything would work out much better." This is nothing less than setting myself up as a god in my own life. I did not believe that what God had given me was truly his best for me.

After my confession, I started to pray for Rita. I thanked and praised God for her. I asked him to give her what was best for her. Slowly my attitude changed.

Finally, instead of using my mouth to devalue my friend, I began to say kind things about her to others. I decided that every word I said about her should be a blessing to her and others. The Lord restored our friendship and taught me an enormous lesson in the process.

Only when a friend feels that we are genuinely rejoicing or mourning with her, rather than feeling jealous and resentful, does she feel safe to share with us her joys and sorrows. This happens when our focus is on her, not on ourselves. When we are secure in our relationship with God and who we are in him, then we are free to embrace the entire gamut of our friend's emotions without any thought for ourselves. Security in our identity in Christ enables us to be a true friend and to create a safe place for our friend.

Gossip

Jealousy is not the only safety hazard that interferes with true friendship. Nothing strips us of a sense of safety faster than gossip.

I don't know whether Rita ever knew that I was saying negative things about her behind her back. If she did, it's no wonder she kept her distance. How could she possibly feel safe in our friendship? She couldn't share her mistakes or struggles with me for fear that I would use this information against her.

True friends do not gossip about one another. The temptation to gossip about a friend indicates that something is amiss in the relationship. And in the initial stages of a friendship, gossip invariably prevents true friendship from developing.

When I am with someone who is saying something negative about a third person, I often think, *I wonder what she says about me when I'm not around.*

If we want to cultivate a true friendship, we need to guard against instigating or participating in gossip. Anything that casts another person in a negative light is better left unsaid. The Bible gives us this simple rule for our speech: "Do not let any unwholesome talk come out of your mouths, but only what is helpful for building others up according to their needs, that it may benefit those who listen" (Eph. 4:29). If we can live by this guideline, others will surely feel safe with us knowing that we will not devalue them to others.

Breaking a Confidence

Closely related to gossip is the practice of breaking a friend's confidence. In other words, our friend shares something with us that is meant for our ears only. We then betray her trust by telling her secret to another friend.

Over a period of several months, Helen had been talking to me about a particular situation in her life. It was a sensitive one, and she counted on me to pray for her and to help her think through the direction she should take. I felt that the others were taking advantage of Helen. But I didn't say that to her. I knew she was loyal to her close friends, and I didn't want to cast a shadow on her other friendships.

So instead of being honest with Helen and keeping my concerns about Helen between me and the Lord, I talked to another friend. I duped myself into thinking I needed a second opinion to validate my own concerns. My other friend offered her insights about Helen's situation.

When Helen called and the topic came up for discussion, I launched into "my" new insights (naturally, not mentioning the fact that they came from another source). But Helen has known me for so long that she recognized that the voice with which I spoke was not my own.

After a long pause, Helen asked, "Ann, did you talk to someone else about this?"

I felt the blood rush to my face. My first impulse was to lie—but I knew I couldn't do that. I had to admit it and apologize.

Helen did not say, "Oh, that's okay." It was not okay. She expressed to me her concern that others would be damaged if this personal information spread to people who knew them. She voiced disappointment that I had broken a confidence. Then she went on to tell me that she loved me and forgave me.

To Helen's credit, she forgave me without hesitation. Not only that, she continued to entrust her personal concerns to me, even after I had so blatantly betrayed her trust. I attribute this to her enormous love for me and the work of the grace of God in her heart.

This experience taught me an important lesson about safeguarding the trust of my friends. When we prove through our actions that we will not leak our friend's secrets, we lay a foundation of trust upon which a true friendship can be built.

Rachel wrote to me about her trusted friend Katrina:

"She protects the trust of our relationship by always treasuring what is shared as though it is for her and no one else. She acts as if what I share is as valuable to her as it is to me. She doesn't share my personal information with her husband unless it involves him or requires his input. All things shared are safe in the treasury of her heart."

None of us will ever achieve perfection in becoming a safe haven for our friends. Just as I failed Helen and still sometimes fail my friends, all of us fall short in this area from time to time. Yet, if we want to have true friendships, we need to examine the patterns in our behavior. If our patterns include jealousy, gossip, and betraying a confidence, then we need to address the behaviors that prevent others from feeling secure with us.

And we all need to set before us goals toward which we can strive. We must set our eyes on Jesus, who was "gentle and humble in heart" (Matt. 11:29) and who can sympathize with our weaknesses (Heb. 4:15). He is the true friend with whom we are totally safe. He urges us to "approach the throne of grace with confidence, so that we may receive mercy and find grace to help us in our time of need" (Heb. 4:16). As we humbly seek him, he will rework the patterns in our lives so that we can become the safe haven—and true friend—we want to be.

Questions for Personal Reflection

1. Read Hebrews 4:15–16 and Matthew 11:28–30. Why are we safe with Jesus? What picture do these verses paint of him?

2. Describe the qualities of gentleness, authenticity, and empathy. Who has demonstrated these to you? How did that make you feel?

3. What safety hazards crop up in your friendships? What can you do about them?

*A friend is a person with
whom I may be sincere.
Before him, I may
think aloud.*

Ralph Waldo Emerson

5   A Listening Ear

I hung up the phone with a mixture of irritation and guilt.

Why do I bother with this 'friendship'? I wondered for the hundredth time.

Kelly and I have known each other for many years. Her three children are just a bit older than my two, and they seem to be turning out perfectly, if such a thing were possible. I suppose that gives Kelly a platform from which to dispense good advice to those of us who have not yet achieved her success. Whenever I am having a problem, Kelly has the solution. From sibling squabbles to housekeeping tips, Kelly has an answer for everything.

Today was no exception. I had been going through a difficult period with one of my teenagers. Kelly knew that the past few months had been more than a bit bumpy. At long last, things seemed to be turning around. I was excited to have good news to share with Kelly.

As I recounted a particularly telling incident to her, Kelly immediately zeroed in on something I had done "wrong." She jumped in and began to tell me what I should and should not have done. Then she shifted the focus of the conversation to herself and her family. I listened as she related the glories of her children and their recent accomplishments.

My glowing victory paled in comparison. In fact, I felt as if it had been completely extinguished, doused by the cold water of her well-intentioned advice.

Yet, I knew Kelly meant to help me. That is why I felt guilty. The fact that it had happened so many times before, yet I kept coming back for more, made me angry at myself as well as angry with Kelly.

Why do I set myself up for this? I fumed to myself. *Every time I tell her anything, I am issuing her an open invitation to tell me what to do! I've simply got to stop telling her anything of importance to me.*

My frustration with Kelly stems in part from the fact that I have spent most of my life doing to others what Kelly does to me. Instead of giving my friends a listening ear, I have advised and corrected. I have turned the conversation back to myself. In short, I have been so self-centered that I have been a very poor listener.

Most of us prefer talking to listening. We automatically focus on ourselves. We want to be understood. We want to be valued. Having someone else listen to us meets our needs. We lose sight of the principle that we should seek "rather to understand than to be understood," to quote the prayer of St. Francis.

Listening, however, is key to developing a true friendship. We can best show a friend that we care by listening to her. Someone has said that listening, not imitation, is the sincerest form of flattery. When we truly listen, we demonstrate that we are interested in what our friend is saying. Conversely, when we do not listen, our actions convey that we are not interested in what she has to say. And that is a relationship killer.

When problems sweep over me and threaten to drown me, my closest friends are my lifeline. What do they do to help? Mostly, they listen. They are there for me on a consistent basis. They do not lecture or launch into accounts of their similar experiences. They listen. In so doing, they manifest to me the presence of Jesus Christ. I need his healing touch, and frequently it comes to me through my friends. Listening is an expression of God's unconditional love.

What Not to Do When Listening

I thought I was a wonderful communicator/listener until I married. As our differences began to surface and Jim explained his viewpoint, I was quick to rush in with a contradictory argument. When we were at a gathering and Jim was telling a story, I interrupted to set the record straight when he had his facts wrong. Before he had a chance to express fully his feelings on a subject, I voiced my own in such strong, dogmatic terms that he backed off the subject entirely.

For many years, I could not understand why my behavior hurt and angered him. I was clueless as to why he increasingly closed himself off from me. Yet, because he loved me and was committed to our marriage, he continued to try to get through to me. My husband lovingly and courageously revealed to me the things that others had never felt at liberty to point out: Some of my communication patterns hurt my relationships.

There, in the mirror of my most honest, intimate relationship, I saw my deficiencies in the listening department. After years of avoiding this uncomplimentary view of myself, I finally looked my reflection squarely in the eye. I recognized wrong behaviors and attitudes. My fears and insecurities caused me to react in a way that shut others down. My dogmatic manner, my arguing and correcting declared me unsafe for self-revelation. If Jim felt this way, surely others did too. I was forced to acknowledge the detrimental effect this was having on all my relationships. I needed to learn to be a better listener.

Wanting to change for the better, I went back to school, figuratively. I majored in listening. Here are some of the lessons I have learned and continue to relearn.

Do Not Interrupt

At my Bible study last week, I interrupted the leader and other group members at least five, if not ten times during the course of our hour together. I kept thinking of funny cracks and jumped in to make them. Everyone laughed. In humor, timing is everything, after all.

But why couldn't I wait until the person speaking completed what she was saying? Was I so full of myself, so desirous of getting a laugh, that I didn't care whom I trampled on in the process?

In a recent conversation with my teenage daughter, she shared with me a moral dilemma one of her friends was facing. This was a tender moment, at bedtime, when she opened up more than usual. Unfortunately, I did not wait for her to disclose her own thoughts on her friend's situation. Instead, I jumped in with my moralistic "Doesn't he know that if he makes that wrong choice, the consequences will be worse in the end?"

Laura frowned. "I know that, Mom. Will you please just listen?"

I realized too late that I had robbed my daughter of the opportunity of sharing with me her own thoughts. I had robbed her of a chance to formulate and develop her moral consciousness. (We all learn best by coming to our own conclusions rather than by hearing someone else's conclusions.) And I had shown her a basic lack of respect.

Whenever we interrupt, we are in essence saying, "What I have to say is more important than what you are saying." That is not the way of love. Love is patient. Love waits for the other person to finish what she has to say. Love does not interrupt.

Do Not Argue

We use the word *contrary* to describe a person who is stubbornly opposed or willful. This behavior stems from various causes including personality, inherent stubbornness, insecurity, and family patterns of argumentativeness. Families can pass this behavior down from generation to generation. If real life has not supplied enough examples of this, television comedies dish it up as daily fare. They depict family members and friends arguing with one another in a way that says, "You dummy! You don't know what you're talking about."

No one likes to be contradicted. It may be funny on television, but it is not pleasant in reality. We tend to avoid people who habitually contradict us, particularly when we are sharing aspects of ourselves—our personal values, thoughts, feelings.

Some people are perfectly comfortable with debate as a style of interaction. For them it may be a contest of wit or words. Certainly there is a time and place for the clashing of differing ideas. In a graduate seminar, a boardroom, or even an amicable exchange of ideas between friends, discussion of opposing views can clarify our thinking and broaden our perspective.

It is very different when the dialogue moves from the realm of ideas to the realm of the personal. I remember a car trip I took with my mother, my aunt, and my uncle when I was in high school. My uncle, a lawyer, enjoys debating. He and I sided against my aunt and my mother in a dispute about whether God originally intended man to be monogamous. He and I argued for polygamy—simply for the sake of argument. For my aunt and my mother, this was not an entertaining exchange. They seemed to take the issue quite a bit more personally than we did.

Call it what you will—argumentativeness, stubbornness, or contentiousness—such behavior squelches disclosure. We learn to stop offering our thoughts and opinions when we know they will be met with an argument.

Note Paul's instruction to his young protégé, Timothy: "Don't have anything to do with foolish and stupid arguments, because you know they produce quarrels. And the Lord's servant must not quarrel; instead, he must be kind to everyone, able to teach, not resentful" (2 Tim. 2:23–24).

Many of us fall into this pattern without realizing it. No matter what our intentions are, argumentativeness is incompatible with good listening skills. If we want to be a true friend, we must become aware of this pattern and stop ourselves midsentence, if need be.

One reason we argue with friends when they share their personal thoughts and feelings is that we think we have a better perspective, a better grasp on the truth, or an insight that our friend lacks. It is natural for us to feel that way, but just because it is natural does not mean it is right. This attitude is erroneous, dangerous, and prideful.

Paul cautions us to "do nothing out of selfish ambition or vain conceit, but in humility consider others better than yourselves" (Phil. 2:3). Humility should temper our responses to our friends. An attitude of humility produces a response of respectful, genuinely interested listening rather than a response of arguing in order to push our own perspective.

Arguing can also stem from fear. We argue because we don't want to consider a viewpoint that is different from our own. We fear that if a loved one voices another opinion, she may act on it, and that action may lead her places we do not want her to go. Yet, true friendship gives a friend the freedom to voice differing opinions and to act on them.

Closely related to fear is insecurity. Often we argue because we feel threatened. We strive to convince our friends to agree with us because we need their agreement to bolster our confidence. Many teenagers exhibit this phenomenon. They contend with their closest friends, sounding absolutely sure of themselves. Yet in reality, they seek uniformity of mind-set. That way, if everyone in the group thinks and feels the same way, the consensus legitimizes their opinions.

I'm not so very different from those teens. Often I make a strong case for an opinion about which I feel uncertain. I want to justify my own behavior or perspective, and I look to my friend to say, "Hmm. I guess you're right." In convincing my friend, I am convinced.

Here fear is at work again. We fear being exposed as wrong. We fear wrestling with an issue that makes us uncomfortable. And most of all, we fear making the changes that the truth would demand, should we be proved wrong.

If we are secure in our own views, and if we trust in a loving and sovereign God, then we need not fear or argue. We can listen in peace, knowing that we and our friend are in God's hands, and truth will prevail in the end.

If we are not secure in our views, we must learn to put aside our personal uncertainties when our friend requires a listening ear. The need to prove ourselves right is a terrible burden. I have learned how freeing it is to say, "You know, I really don't know how I feel about that." When we can be honest with ourselves and our friends about our own ambiguities, we release ourselves from bondage to anxiety. Relaxed in the knowledge that we don't have to have all the answers, we are freed up to listen to our friend's point of view.

Do Not Correct

This brings us to a similar bad habit: correcting, or setting others straight. Born of arrogance, this behavior is particularly lethal to friendship. When we correct another, we assume a position of superiority. It presupposes that we have a corner on the truth.

A wise person once told me, "It is more important to be kind than to be correct." I try to remember this when someone is relating a story and has some of the details wrong. I'm tempted to interject the correct information. Then I recall these wise words and remind myself that it doesn't really matter if my friend has some extraneous details wrong. What matters is that I show love and consideration to the one who is telling the story.

My friend Missy struggled with a number of personal issues over a period of several years. During some especially dark times of hopelessness, she questioned God's goodness and his loving purposes for her life. At first I felt it was my responsibility to "set her straight." Her theology was all wrong!

My theology lessons didn't seem to help Missy. In fact, they made things worse. On top of her own despair, she felt I misunderstood and looked down on her. This only increased her pain. And I became more and more frustrated when she didn't accept my "helpful insights." My frustration surfaced in impatience and anger.

It took me a long time to learn that she did not need to be corrected, nor did my correction help her one bit. What she needed was a loving, sympathetic listener. I am thankful Missy did not give up on me before I learned this important lesson.

Do Not Try to Solve a Friend's Problems

I made another mistake with Missy. I tried to solve her problems. Every time she unburdened herself with me, I proposed helpful suggestions that, if heeded, would prevent her from ending up in the slough of despond. Or so I thought. As month followed month, and the same problems kept recurring, I became increasingly frustrated. If she would only just do what I said!

As is true in most cases, her problems were not that simple. And my continual posing of solutions only exacerbated her despair. My behavior reinforced her feelings of self-doubt.

Repeatedly she said to me, "Ann, I don't need you to solve my problems. I just need for you to listen." When I began to heed these wise words, things began to change. I no longer felt responsible for Missy's happiness. I realized I was not called to be her savior. I was simply a friend, there to listen and show her I cared.

Missy began to feel less like my project and more like my peer. A new sense of freedom pervaded our friendship. I no longer felt weighed down by her problems. She no longer felt pressured to perform for my approval. The secret lay in my giving up my need to rescue her.

That does not mean we should never give advice. There is a time to give wise, thoughtful advice, but that time is later in the course of the friendship, and only after many, many hours of listening.

Listening is a humble posture. It does not assume that we have divine insight into our friend's situation. We gain insight as we walk the miles of friendship together, listening and observing our friend under all conditions. Long and careful listening allows us to provide wise advice at a later stage.

Do Not Use One-Upmanship

Suppose we have wonderful news that we are eager to share with a friend, but when she hears it, she immediately launches into some even more glorious news of her own. Or we have had a hard week and call a friend for some sympathy. Instead, she regales us with how much more horrendous her week has been. This is one-upmanship.

Mothers of young children love to swap horror stories about sleep deprivation and the overwhelming nature of life with babies and toddlers. When bleary-eyed, frazzled young mothers would complain to me, I used to love to tell the story of another friend who had twin boys. When her twins were only a year and a half old, she then discovered she was pregnant again. This time it was triplets— and they were all boys! She had five boys ages two and under! That invariably got a reaction.

It took me many years to realize that my impressive stories were less than helpful. While she was reacting with amazement, my frazzled friend was thinking, *Wow. I only have two kids, and I can't cope. What's wrong with me?*

My desire to impress was nothing short of self-gratification. Competing for sympathy or praise may come naturally, but it does not show the love of Jesus Christ.

> Your attitude should be the same as that of Christ Jesus:
> Who, being in very nature God,
>> did not consider equality with God something to be grasped,
> but made himself nothing,
>> taking the very nature of a servant,
>> being made in human likeness.
> And being found in appearance as a man,
>> he humbled himself
>> and became obedient to death—even death on a cross!
>> Philippians 2:5–8

Listening is a way of adopting Christ's attitude. We should "rejoice with those who rejoice; mourn with those who mourn" (Rom. 12:15). If our aim is to love our friend, we will keep our bigger-and-better stories to ourselves. Instead, we will show sympathy and concern for our friend and allow the focus to remain on her.

A New Mind-Set

Becoming a better listener is not simply a matter of adopting a set of behaviors. Attitude is key. Our listening

habits flow from our attitudes. Bad listening habits eman-
ate from attitudes of self-aggrandizement, self-absorption,
and self-promotion. Good listening patterns flow out of
an attitude of genuine interest in and love for the other
person.

Here are some specific attitudes to embrace when striving to become a better listener.

An Attitude of Understanding

If we are a good listener, we seek first and foremost to
understand our friend. We endeavor to perceive what our
friend is feeling and why. We glean clues from her history,
personality, and reactions. It is, in fact, very much like de-
tective work. Our hours of careful, observant listening
enable us to piece together a fairly accurate picture of the
inner workings of our friend. This happens when the goal is
understanding.

An Attitude of Reserved Judgment

If we are truly seeking to understand our friend, then we
do not approach her with a critical attitude. Instead, we
decide we will give her the benefit of the doubt. We reserve
judgment while we gather all the facts.

There may come a time when the facts inevitably lead
us to a judgment, and that judgment may require words or
action on our part. That time, however, is after the facts
are in and we have given the matter much prayerful consideration. It takes place after we have proven our love over
time through our actions.

In the meantime, love necessitates that we keep ourselves from jumping to conclusions or rushing to formulate an opinion before hearing the complete story. Need I
add that the complete story rarely unfolds in one sitting?
Every story has many hidden facets that come to light only
with time and through nonjudgmental listening.

An Attitude of Respect

If we hold our friend in high esteem, we are guaranteed to be better listeners. Several years ago John R. W. Stott visited our church and delivered messages on the crucifixion and resurrection. I eagerly anticipated his coming. Ever since I was a college student active in Inter-Varsity Christian Fellowship, I have been blessed by his writing and teaching ministry. When he spoke, I hung on his every word. My respect for him sharpened my listening skills.

Our friend may not be a world-renowned writer and speaker, but she is made in the image of God. And if she believes in Jesus Christ, then she is a part of his body on earth. Is she any less worthy of our esteem?

Jesus said, "I tell you the truth, whatever you did for one of the least of these brothers of mine, you did for me" (Matt. 25:40). We are to treat our friend just as if she were Jesus. That means we listen with a sense of respect.

A New Set of Behaviors

This new mind-set manifests itself in tangible ways—in a new set of behaviors. We look our friend in the eyes and keep our eyes trained on her as she speaks. Wandering eyes betray lack of interest. We nod as she speaks to show we are following what she is saying.

Our words confirm that we are truly listening. We say things like "That must be so painful." Our words acknowledge her feelings. We ask careful, nonjudgmental questions to draw our friend out and help her explore her own thoughts and feelings.

We give her a hug when her eyes well up with tears. The next time we see her or speak with her privately, we ask specifically about her concerns. This demonstrates that we care enough to remember. Everything about our behavior signals caring.

In Dietrich Bonhoeffer's classic work on the body of Christ, *Life Together,* he wrote about the ministry of listening:

> The first service that one owes to others in the fellowship consists in listening to them. Just as love to God begins with listening to His Word, so the beginning of love for the brethren is learning to listen to them. It is God's love for us that He not only gives us His Word but also lends us His ear. So it is His work that we do for our brother when we learn to listen to him. Christians . . . forget that listening can be a greater service than speaking.
>
> Many people are looking for an ear that will listen. They do not find it among Christians, because these Christians are talking when they should be listening. But he who can no longer listen to his brother will soon no longer be listening to God either; he will be doing nothing but prattle in the presence of God too. Anyone who thinks that his time is too valuable to spend keeping quiet will eventually have no time for God and his brother, but only for himself and his own follies.
>
> There is a kind of listening with half an ear that presumes already to know what the other person has to say. It is an impatient, inattentive listening, that despises the brother and is only waiting for a chance to speak. . . . It is little wonder that we are no longer capable of the greatest service of listening that God has committed to us, that of hearing our brother's confession, if we refuse to give ear to our brother on lesser subjects. Secular education today is aware that often a person can be helped merely by having someone who will listen to him seriously, and upon this insight it has constructed its own soul therapy, which has attracted great numbers of people. . . . But Christians have forgotten that the ministry of listening has been committed to them by Him who is Himself the great listener and whose work they should share.[1]

Jesus set an example as a listener par excellence. He never put anyone off because he was preoccupied with his own concerns. He never interrupted. He never put words in others' mouths. Rather, he listened so well that he perceived the deeper issues at hand. His listening gave dignity to small children, outcast women, and ostracized lepers. No wonder multitudes flocked to him!

Do you know someone with a special gift for listening? It truly is a ministry, but one that does not require unique gifts or a dramatic calling. We are all called to the ministry of listening because it expresses the love of Jesus Christ. By simply listening, we can be an agent of healing. Listening brings balm to the wounded, clarity to the confused, and renewed strength to the weary.

Few people are naturally good listeners. By nature, we are all self-centered. Yet, becoming a true friend involves getting the focus off ourself and onto the other person.

Listening shifts our focus to our friend. By saying no to our urges to interrupt or solve our friend's problem, we lay down our life for our friend in small but very real ways. As we listen to our friend, we sacrifice ourself and give her a precious gift that sets us on the road to a treasured friendship.

Questions for Personal Reflection

1. What bad habits prevent you from being a good listener?

2. What changes do you desire to make in your attitudes and behaviors regarding listening?

3. Meditate on Philippians 2:3–8. How does this apply to the subject of listening to one's friend?

A friend should bear his friend's infirmities.

Shakespeare

The Strong Arms of a Friend

6

When my husband, Steve, was diagnosed with kidney cancer a year ago, Claire was there to pick me up off the floor and help me get through it," Yvonne told me. "She cared for my children, helped with meals, and carpooled my kids around while I stayed with my husband. Three days after Steve's surgery, our daughter broke her arm. Claire sat with Steve in the hospital while I was in the emergency room with Melissa having her cast made. When I brought Melissa up to Steve's room and put her in the other bed, Claire took me to dinner while they slept.

"As if that weren't enough, three weeks later our eighteen-year-old son got into very serious trouble with the law. My husband was home and mending by then. We were on TV and in the newspapers. Everyone knew the seriousness of what happened. Again Claire came, ripped the covers off my head, and dragged me out of bed.

"While we were dealing with all of this, my father had open heart surgery in Southern California. I couldn't be with him because our son was coming home from his (thankfully) short time in jail. When my father died after his surgery, it was Claire who came and, with Jesus' love, helped me get through it.

"I call this year my Job year. But unlike Job, I had a great friend who loved me and cared for me. Without her help and support, our family would not have gotten through it all. Because of her, we are still able to laugh, and we have the most precious friend God has given anyone."

Claire was there for her friend Yvonne. Without waiting to be asked, she sensed and supplied exactly what Yvonne needed at every new twist in the road.

True friends are the people we know we can count on when the bottom falls out of our life. Why? Because they continue to demonstrate the love Jesus taught and lived— the love that makes it possible for a person to lay down her life for a friend.

Love in Action

True friends delight in giving of themselves to one another. This is the natural outflow of a heart brimming over with love. As in any love relationship, true friendship manifests itself in action.

The apostle John wrote, "Dear children, let us not love with words or tongue but with actions and in truth" (1 John 3:18). Whether a friendship is a true friendship depends on whether loving actions characterize the relationship. True friendship is about helping one another.

A friend who is single tells me that she knows who her real friends are: They're the ones she feels she can ask to take her to the airport. Think about it. We all hate to inconvenience others. None of us relishes being a burden to others. When we have a need, like getting to or from the airport, we call on family members or friends who will not regard this as a burden. Because they love us, they are happy to perform this service. And they know we will do the same for them.

Yet, in a society that venerates self-reliance as ours does, most of us balk at calling on others for anything. We think we are being considerate of others, not wanting to take advantage of their goodwill. We want to "save them for an emergency," to quote one friend of mine.

The problem is that when the emergency comes, if we have not been involved in giving to and receiving from friends, we will not be close enough to them to ask them for help. When the big crises hit, we turn to those who have helped us all along in little ways. Refusing help isolates us from others. Accepting help from others knits our lives together with theirs.

A true friend counts it a privilege to give of herself. It is a way of saying, "I care about you. I'll always be there for you."

When a crisis comes, many people say they want to help, and most of them sincerely do. In the midst of a crisis, however, we don't have the energy or ability to direct our friends in how best to help us. A true friend will try to discover what is most needed.

Several years ago, Cary learned that she had breast cancer. She faced several surgeries, radiation, and chemotherapy. She worried about how she would run her household and care for her two preschool children.

Up stepped her close friend Amy. Amy took over the job of organizing all Cary's meals, child care, and errands. A whiz with the computer, Amy created a database with the names and telephone numbers of everyone who offered to help. She made telephone calls, coordinated schedules, and gave Cary a computer printout of what was happening when. That way Cary did not need to call those offering assistance. Instead, she could channel her precious strength into healing her body and loving her family.

Many wonderful friends pitched in to help Cary during her treatment. One person deposited bread and homegrown tomatoes (Cary's favorite) on her front doorstep on a regular basis with no name attached. Someone else delivered two week's worth of school lunches, all bagged and labeled with each child's name. In addition to food, each bag held stickers and surprises. Some friends ran errands for Cary, including returning dishes to people who brought meals in nondisposable containers. One friend who is gifted in sewing constructed items of clothing for Cary to wear in the hospital, especially suited to meet her particular needs. Still another friend offered her services as a shopping consultant. She went with Cary to help her select a lovely nightgown and robe for her hospital stays. One friend planted tulips and crocuses in Cary's garden in the fall so that Cary could be cheered by bright, colorful flowers in the early spring.

The list goes on. Countless friends showered Cary with deeds of kindness, support, and care during her time of great need. Amy's organizational abilities facilitated this. Her willingness to be the "point man" blessed Cary and made it possible for all of Cary's friends to help her in a tangible way that eased her burden and met the need of the hour. Cary said, "If not for Amy's organization, lots of offers would have gone unused because of my difficulty in calling back to say, 'Can you bring me some food?' Amy went way beyond the call of normal friendship."

I'm sure there was a cost involved for Amy. She was not sitting at home twiddling her thumbs before she got wind of Cary's diagnosis. Amy, like Cary, is a young, vibrant Christian woman, a wife and a mother of several young children. She plunges into activities with great commitment and enthusiasm be it at church, in the community, or at her children's school. Amy had to lay aside some of her own interests and other commitments when she made herself available to Cary.

Jesus defined love this way: "Greater love has no one than this, that he lay down his life for his friends" (John

15:13). Amy laid down her life for Cary by giving up her time, her energy, even some of her obligations in order to help her friend.

Know Your Limitations

Right about now, you may be feeling guilty. You remember times when a friend was going through a hard time, yet you were so immersed in your own problems that you did not reach out to her. Your circumstances conspired to render you useless to her in her time of need.

The truth is we all have factors in our lives that limit our ability and availability to help our friends. But we must remember that the very circumstances that seem to stand in the way of showing God's love are sent to us by our loving heavenly Father.

Certainly our families are God-given limitations. As a wife and a mother, my primary responsibilities are to love my husband and to love and care for my children. They can fend for themselves on an occasional basis while I am off helping a friend. In fact, that is good for them. Yet, I shirk my divine calling if I desert them on a regular or long-term basis.

Often our family members shrink from telling us they need more of us, especially when they see we are busy doing good deeds for others. It feels selfish to say, "Honey, when do I get time to talk to you or enjoy being with you?" Small children cannot articulate these feelings. They simply become unhappy. Then they act out in some way. We don't realize they are feeling neglected until we get a phone call from their teacher at school reporting an escalation in misdeeds in the classroom and on the playground.

Because I place a high value on friendship, I can easily slip into a pattern of putting my friends' needs before the needs of my family. On several occasions, my husband has had to say to me, "Ann, we need you too." My attention or lack of attention has a profound effect on my husband and our children. No one else can fill my shoes as wife and mother.

Special circumstances with extended family can also limit our availability. Parents with declining health require our time and an enormous amount of emotional energy. A chronically ill or physically challenged family member needs our love, our time, and our attention. We minister to Jesus Christ when we fulfill our family obligations to ones such as these. Jesus said, "Whatever you did for one of the least of these brothers of mine, you did for me" (Matt. 25:40). Family crises render us less available to help needy friends, but we must not neglect the family members God has put in our care.

Some women face physical limitations. Sheri is one of the most generous women I know. Until two years ago, she was always the first to deliver a full, hot meal to every woman from church who had just had a baby. Using her gift for hospitality, she often housed missionaries, friends from out of town, or a friend from church who was hurting and needed a place of shelter. Then one day Sheri was in a terrible automobile accident. Fortunately, her life was spared. She went through a horrific ordeal of three surgeries and physical therapy that restored many of her capabilities. But she now lives in chronic pain and must restrict her activity severely.

"I keep trying to do too much, but then my family and I pay a price," Sheri confided. "It has been very humbling to realize that I physically cannot help others in the way I did before the accident. Yet, I have had to learn to trust God in this, that even these limitations come from my gracious Father's hand."

You alone know the boundaries within which you must operate. You must address these honestly with God in prayer. God gives us limitations for our own safety. If we had none, we might feel constrained to be all things to all people. We cannot do that. We simply cannot be true friends to everyone.

If we accept our limitations and joyfully seek to serve our friends and loved ones to the best of our ability within these parameters, God will bless our endeavors. When we offer the little we have to God, he has promised to multiply it.

Jesus said, "Give, and it will be given to you. A good measure, pressed down, shaken together and running over, will be poured into your lap. For with the measure you use, it will be measured to you" (Luke 6:38). The same Jesus who multiplied the loaves and the fishes will take our limited resources and multiply the blessings in the lives of the friends we serve.

Are you a serve-until-you-drop type? Or do you guard your boundaries to the point of stinginess? I find that most women fall into one category or the other.

If you serve your friends relentlessly until your family suffers and you are a nervous wreck, then you need to learn to live within your limitations. Expect to feel wracked with guilt the first several times you don't offer your services. Everything within you will be screaming to swoop down and do things for the person in need. Any change in our typical pattern is extremely uncomfortable, especially when it feels like we are being cold, unloving, or selfish. As you squirm in anguish, simply remind yourself that you need to step aside so that God can tap others on the shoulder to help. If you do everything, you rob others of the opportunity to be blessed by helping. And you are not being selfish by fulfilling your God-given responsibilities and living by his priorities.

On the other hand, if you rarely help a friend because you are absorbed with your own family, job, and so on, perhaps you need to extend yourself a bit more. As long as we don't overdo it, we actually do our families a favor by turning our focus outward on a regular basis. Our children need to see us exemplify generosity and kindness, faithfulness and commitment. Additionally, an occasional shift in attention provides our families with some much-needed breathing room. If Mom is always hovering, the children never stretch their wings. They remain too dependent on us rather than learning to be independent, which is our ultimate goal in parenting.

When Helping Doesn't Help

This issue of dependency also enters into the arena of helping friends. At times our well-intentioned efforts to help friends actually hurt them by fostering their dependency on us.

When Kate slid into a deep depression, Suzanne stepped in to help. She cleaned Kate's house and laundered her clothes. She brought her meals. She sat with her, holding her hand and encouraging her. Suzanne removed all of Kate's medications from her house so that Kate would not be tempted to take an overdose. Suzanne even ran interference for Kate, trying to protect her from experiencing failure or hearing negative things that could push her further into her depression.

Strangely enough, the more Suzanne did, the worse Kate's depression became. Suzanne loved Kate very much and meant to help her. All her efforts only served to convince Kate that she was incapable of coping with her life. Not forced to function, Kate curled up in her cocoon and succumbed to passivity.

Before long, Suzanne exhausted herself with this tremendous burden. She felt not only depleted but also confused. Instead of being grateful, Kate reacted with resentment. Obviously something was going wrong. Suzanne began to seek God in prayer and seek the advice of godly counselors.

She realized before it was too late that Kate needed her love and support, but she did not need Suzanne to do everything for her. Only when Kate assumed responsibility for her own life did she begin to progress toward normalcy.

Suzanne learned that she had been doing something that psychologists call *overfunctioning*. This spawned a natural reaction of underfunctioning in Kate. Overfunctioning involves doing things for others that they are capable of doing for themselves. It involves feeling responsible for others and feeling as though we know what is best for them. Overfunctioning manifests itself in worrying and excessive advice-giving.

Underfunctioning, on the other hand, manifests itself in asking for advice instead of thinking things through independently, acting irresponsibly, either not formulating goals or formulating them without following through, getting others to help when help is not really needed, and becoming mentally and physically ill frequently.

When we overfunction in our friends' lives, we do not help them. Yet, when someone I love underfunctions, I find it almost impossible not to overfunction. It hurts to see my loved one make choices, actively or passively, that seem to me to be bad ones. I think, *She's in trouble. She needs my help. I can't just sit by and watch her self-destruct.*

So I rush in where angels fear to tread. I assume that I know what is best for my friend, and I set about with considerable vigor to accomplish it. Then to my dismay I discover that my efforts seem to be producing a negative effect. The more I do to help, the less my friend does to make necessary, responsible changes in her life. It is a vicious cycle that spirals downward with increasing velocity.

Worse still, by overfunctioning, we sabotage God's work in our friend's life. God may have guided our friend into a dark valley on purpose. Or he may be allowing her to experience the consequences of wrong choices. Only in the pitch darkness will she come face to face with her fears,

failures, and sins, and cry out to God for help. If we keep
sending in blankets and flashlights, we enable her to remain in the darkness rather than to seek the One True
Light who casts out all darkness.

How do we break the overfunction/underfunction cycle
in a friendship? Our first priority is to ensure that we ourselves are growing in a vital relationship with Jesus Christ.
Only as he daily refreshes our spirit, fills us with his wisdom, and energizes us with his strength are we able to have
anything at all to give our friend. I love 2 Peter 1:3, which
promises, "His divine power has given us everything we
need for life and godliness through our knowledge of him
who called us by his own glory and goodness." He will
show us what we should or should not do to help, and he
will supply us with the strength of body and will to obey.

We must simply stop trying to protect our friend from
the consequences of her choices. Only then can our hurting friend assume responsibility for her choices and for her
own relationship with the Lord. Believe me, it will take
courage to refrain from jumping in when you see your
friend flounder. Every cell in your body will be shouting
to intervene. Yet, as my friend Linda said to me, "Laying
down your life sometimes means not doing the very thing
that everything in you aches to do to help."

Essentially, the decision not to rescue often boils down
to trusting God. It is prideful to think, *My friend's well-being
depends on me.* To refrain from overfunctioning requires
that we entrust our friend to God. We must believe that God
loves our friend more than we do and that he is working in
her life according to his sovereign, benevolent purposes.

To Help or Not to Help

That is not to say that God does not use us in our friends'
lives. We certainly do not want to be like the priest and

the Levite who passed by the half-dead man in Jesus' parable of the good Samaritan (Luke 10:30–35). Jesus used this story about the despised Samaritan who stopped on his journey to provide care for a hurting man in order to define what is meant by loving your neighbor. Love means reaching out in mercy to the one who needs help.

But how do we know when we are being helpful and when we are overfunctioning? This question can paralyze us. There are no easy answers to this complex dilemma. I have no slick formula to offer. But here are some suggestions that may help us find our way as we seek to obey God and love our friend.

Pray

Too often I rush to action before stopping to pray. I follow my instincts instead of following the leading of the Holy Spirit. My friend Linda describes it thus: "Our feeling is so strong that we don't even inquire of the Lord about it. We end up doing something in Jesus' name that is really counter to God's plan for our friend."

In our private prayers, we must take our friend's situation before God and ask him what, if anything, he would have us do. Then we must wait and see how God leads. This more measured approach might well prevent much meddling that masquerades as helping.

Similarly, if our friend is a Christian, we should pray with her about her problem. Linda continued, "In this way, we point our friends to Jesus. Our friends need to know that it is God who provides for their needs. Pray together, and together wait on God."

Ask Questions

We should question our motivation. Ask, *Why do I want to help?* Often we become involved in "rescue missions" because it makes us feel significant, not because our primary concern is for our friend's well-being. Or sometimes we eagerly immerse ourselves in others' problems as a way of running away from uncomfortable issues of our own closer to home.

Perhaps we need to ask, *Why don't I want to help?* Is it really because our other commitments require all our time? Or is it because we become uncomfortable in messy situations that are time-consuming, inconvenient, or make us feel inadequate?

Most of the time, we are motivated by genuine love and concern for our friend. Compassion compels us to alleviate our friend's suffering. We must remember, however, that suffering is the very instrument that God most often uses to draw us to himself. It could be that our friend must experience the full brunt of the suffering in order to make significant changes in her life and her relationship with God.

We should ask, *What is most helpful to my friend?* We should not necessarily take our friend's word for it. When we are hurting, what we think we need frequently differs from what we truly need. Ultimately, we cannot answer that question. God alone knows what our friend needs. We must continue to seek God's guidance as to what our role should be in helping our friend. That brings us back to prayer and ahead to seeking godly counsel.

Seek Godly Counsel

Do you have a wise, spiritually mature friend who knows you well but does not know your other friend? Go to her and share your dilemma. Be careful not to divulge details that would betray your friend's confidence. Remember that the focus here is not on your friend's situation but on you, on your heart, on what God would have you do.

If our friend is in serious trouble, after first going to her with our concerns, we should seek the counsel of our minister or hers. Her pastor may know more about her situation than we do and may be able to direct us so that our efforts help and don't exacerbate her troubles. On more than one occasion I have called on a professional counselor who volunteers with our church's pastoral care team. Her insights have proved invaluable, guiding me in how best to help my friend.

Watch for Signs of Underfunctioning

If our friend seems to be getting less responsible instead of more, this is a definite red flag. If she seems to be requiring more assistance and looking to us more for advice, direction, and goals, then we are not helping her by supplying these things.

Reevaluate

Our ultimate purpose in helping our friend is to demonstrate Christ's love in such a way that she sees him and responds to him, on her own. She must make her own choices. In the final analysis, she will live with their consequences. If she is not being helped by our efforts on her behalf, it's time to go back to the drawing board—or the kneeling bench.

For Everything a Season . . .

Early in his naval career, my walking group leader, J. P., served aboard an American naval vessel carrying marines up the Yangtze River in China during World War II. They came upon a capsized Chinese boat. The men in the boat must have been carrying cabbages to market, for cabbages bobbed in the water alongside the drowning men. A second Chinese boat floated among the men and cabbages.

The men aboard this second vessel crouched over the side of their boat holding scooplike nets. Imagine the American sailors' shock when they discovered that the men in the second boat were scooping out the cabbages and leaving the men to drown!

The Americans went to work rescuing the drowning Chinese men. They hauled them all aboard and provided dry clothing and good food. Before long, the Americans had another problem. The Chinese had never had it so good. When the Americans came into port, the Chinese refused to get off the ship. The captain had to send for the Chinese police to board the vessel and forcibly remove the men from the ship.

Wise King Solomon wrote: "There is a time for everything, and a season for every activity under heaven: a time to be born and a time to die, a time to plant and a time to uproot . . ." (Eccles. 3:1–2). You might add "a time to rescue drowning men and a time to call the police to haul them off your ship."

When a friend is drowning, we cannot turn a blind eye and continue fishing for cabbages! We must put out our hand and draw our friend out of the water. Yet, the friend is rescued from death to live her own life, not to live aboard our ship.

True friendship is a matter of mutual give and take. We will all encounter times when we feel like those poor men flailing around in the Yangtze River. At times like this, we desperately need friends to pull us out. And we will all experience times when a friend is drowning. Then it is our turn to help.

A true friend gives freely when her friend needs help, and she receives gladly when she is in need. No one keeps score in a true friendship, yet somehow the giving and receiving balances out. May God give us the wisdom, strength, and grace both to give and to receive in a way that helps our friend and honors Jesus Christ.

Questions
for Personal
Reflection

1. Identify a true friend who demonstrated extraordinary love when you were in need. What did you find especially helpful?

2. What are your limitations? Do you need to learn to live within them or do you need to extend yourself more for your friends? How can you go about making these changes?

3. Read the story of the good Samaritan in Luke 10:25–37. How does this apply to true friendship? How do you determine when to help and when to refrain from helping?

*This communicating of a
man's self to his friend works
two contrary effects, for it
redoubleth joys, and cutteth
griefs in half.*

Francis Bacon

7 The Power of Encouragement

When Noreene awoke on the morning of her birthday, depression washed over her with its broad brush stroke of gray. Normally, Noreene is irrepressibly fun-loving, always game for a good time. But work pressures had begun to choke all the pleasure out of her life. Sleep eluded her at night, and anxiety shrouded her days. She went through the motions of her morning routine, preparing for her daily walk with our group.

She opened the front door to be greeted by the loud honking of party horns and the screeching of party noisemakers. J. P. and I stood in her front yard wearing shimmering top hats, holding brightly colored, helium-filled balloons, and blowing our horns for all we were worth. Noreene dissolved into gales of laughter.

We adorned her head with a huge Mexican sombrero (Noreene spent many years in Mexico and loves all things Mexican), tied the balloon strings to her wrist, and set out for our walk. From one end of our town to the other, we traversed the bike path in full party regalia. Every time we met someone on the path, we blew our horns and sounded our noisemakers. Some asked us, "What's the occasion?" Others wondered if we had been partying all night and were just on our way home. The grumpy ones simply ignored us.

We stopped in at a coffee shop, where groggy business-people shot us alarmed looks. "Who are these weirdos?" their glances said. "Perhaps they have already had too much caffeine?" We laughed the entire duration of our walk.

As we parted, Noreene turned and hugged each of us. "I was expecting a pretty grim birthday," she admitted. "I never expected this. You guys are the greatest—you've really cheered me up. You've given me a birthday I'll never forget!"

Noreene's problems did not disappear. Our birthday extravaganza could not erase them. But it did help her to escape from their pressure for a two-hour respite. Laughter lifted her spirits and buoyed her strength to tackle the day. More important, our deed of thoughtfulness and our continuing, committed, and caring presence in her life encouraged her in a way that carried her through her birthday and the weeks and months that followed.

True friends encourage one another. This is a very important function of friendship. Almost every day brings irritations, setbacks, hassles, and frustrations. Those little, negative things can get us down if we don't have the positive force of friendship to counterbalance them.

As if the little things aren't enough, sooner or later we encounter big problems: heartbreaking sorrows, bitter disappointments, gripping fear. No one escapes these things in life. Pain is part and parcel to life in a sin-wracked world. At times such as these, we desperately need true friends to give us the courage to persevere.

King Solomon painted a vivid picture of the encouragement of true friendship in Ecclesiastes 4:9–12:

> Two are better than one,
>> because they have a good return for their work:
> If one falls down,
>> his friend can help him up.

But pity the man who falls
   and has no one to help him up!
Also, if two lie down together, they will keep warm.
   But how can one keep warm alone?
Though one may be overpowered,
   two can defend themselves.
A cord of three strands is not quickly broken.

We encourage our friend by helping her up when she has stumbled and fallen. We encourage our friend by encircling her with our warmth when she is chilled. We encourage our friend by being with her so that she does not face the wolves alone. Through the power of encouragement, true friends are stronger together than the combination of their individual strengths. The whole is greater than the sum of its parts.

What Is Encouragement?

The *Merriam Webster's Collegiate Dictionary* defines *encourage* in this way: 1. to inspire with courage, spirit, or hope. 2. to spur on. 3. to give help or patronage to.

This means that my life produces a positive effect on my friend. She is stronger, more courageous, more confident, better focused because of me and our friendship.

Most of us want to have a positive impact on our friends. We want them to be the better for our friendship. But how? How can we be an encouragement to our friends?

Encouragement through Laughter

Smiles and laughter go a long way toward heartening our friends. Just as our walking group's silly birthday buffoonery perked up Noreene's spirits, so also we can use laughter on a daily basis to encourage those around us.

Most of us love to laugh, and we are attracted to people who see the humor in life. When I reflect on all my close friendships throughout my life, I see one common thread—a sense of humor. All my friends have been a little wild and crazy, some more than others.

On a recent trip to California, I met Meg, an attractive redheaded woman whose wide smile and dancing eyes revealed a personality of gusto and good humor. After I spoke about not using one-upmanship in friendship, she said, "My friend Sally and I have this one-upmanship game that we play all the time, just for fun. For instance, if I say, 'I've got corns on my toes,' my friend will shoot back, 'Well, I'm going to have to have my toes amputated!'

"We laugh together all the time. Both of us have gone through painful family situations over the past few years, and we couldn't have made it alone. Laughing together helped a lot. Plus we were just there for each other."

Laughter is good for us. Proverbs 17:22 tells us, "A cheerful heart is good medicine." We have all experienced the medicinal value of laughter.

The best comedy occurs naturally in the warp and woof of life. Small children provide humor on a daily basis. Grab a pen and write down that funny line your child just said. Write it on a napkin, the calendar, anywhere so that you won't forget it before you talk to your friend.

My friend Martha constantly has me in stitches because of her propensity for merging cliches. She routinely mis-uses colloquialisms with Dickensian flair. Some of my favorites include "Wake up and smell the roses," "I'm shooting myself in the hip," and "creme de la crop." She doesn't intend to do this, but she finds her turns of phrase as funny as I do. Now I collect "Marthaisms," as I call them.

Humor can be found in the most mundane details of life. Some people see it quite readily. Others must consciously look for it. If we want to uplift our friends, we do well to cultivate our lighter side.

Here are some ways I bring humor into my life and friendships. Although I rarely read the newspaper, I do make a point of reading the comics. Often, when a strip reminds me of a friend or I know she would really appreciate the humor, I cut it out and give it to her. For several years, I sent Dave Barry's weekly humor column to a long-distance friend. We joked about my giving her "humor therapy." When I hear a funny story, I try to tell it right away or write it down and file it in my "humor" file. (Those of us with deficient memories must compensate by being organized!)

Cruise secondhand stores and yard sales for an old joke book. (Make sure the humor is in good taste before you buy, however!) Place it in the bathroom or on a table in the family room. There you will be sure to glance through it from time to time, gleaning a few good jokes to pass on to friends. We don't need to be stand-up comedians to enjoy humor and share it with a friend. As we develop our capacity for humor, we add refreshing zest to our friendships.

As therapeutic as humor is, however, it can also be destructive. Be careful. Never use humor to put down another person or to belittle your friend's problems. Without doubt, there is a time to laugh and a time to refrain from laughter. The latter requires that we encourage our friend in other ways.

Encouragement by Our Presence

Sometimes all it takes to comfort us is the presence of a friend, as shown in the story Melinda told me:

"When I was a junior in college, my fiancé called off our wedding. I was devastated. My friend Mindy was there for me, comforting me with her presence at a time when I needed someone to lean on. She spent the entire day with me—crying with me, listening to me, sharing my pain. She did not offer advice. She did not try to tell me that everything would be okay, that God had a plan for my life, and that I would get through this. There would be time for that later, when I was ready to hear those words. Mindy knew I was not ready and that I needed time to grieve. Her presence that day and in the days and months that followed gave me strength and encouragement. Looking back on the experience, I know that God used Mindy in a special way to help me through a painful time in my life and to help me heal."

If we want to inspire courage in our friend (as the dictionary defines *encourage*), this is often best done by offering our presence. Just as a frightened child finds her fears dispelled when her mother enters the room, we take comfort from the loving presence of our friends.

This is especially true in times of deep grief. Our grieving friends need our presence, not our words. Words are lame in moments such as these. They too easily wound the heart laid bare by loss. It is far better simply to "keep watch" with our friend.

When Job lost his family, his property, and his health, his three friends came to be with him. Job 2:11–13 tells us,

> When Job's three friends, Eliphaz the Temanite, Bildad the Shuhite and Zophar the Naamathite, heard about all the troubles that had come upon him, they set out from their homes and met together by agreement to go and sympathize with him and comfort him. When they saw him from a distance, they could hardly recognize him; they began to weep aloud, and they tore their robes and sprinkled dust on their heads. Then they sat on the ground with him for seven days and seven nights. No one said a word to him, because they saw how great his suffering was.

Then they made the mistake of opening their mouths. In the end, when God spoke, he condemned Job's friends for offering their well-intentioned explanations and advice.

They would have encouraged Job, rather than discouraged him, if they had continued to sit with him in silence.

Encouragement through Synergism

Our presence does more than simply bring comfort when our friend is suffering. Our presence also works actively to inspire and motivate our friend, as we cheer her on with our words.

Nancy, a young woman from Wisconsin, shared with me an example of this kind of encouragement:

"Joan, a former college roommate, and I decided to take on a major challenge: ski the American Birkebeiner, a thirty-three mile international cross-country ski race in Cable, Wisconsin. Neither of us was an athlete; we didn't do it to compete, just to complete it! We spent a month in training—pushing, encouraging, and challenging each other. Many times one of us would want to give up, but the other would keep her going. My friend Joan put it this way: 'I can stretch beyond myself because you are pulling on one end.' That's what true friendships do. They stretch us, push us, pull us, support us. They enable us to do things we could never do alone, to be women we could never be on our own."

This is the principle of synergism in which "the interaction of elements when combined produces a total effect that is greater than the sum of the individual elements." Nancy continued, "Two people working together can accomplish more than two people working individually. We need each other to accomplish God's purposes in our lives."

If this is true when we undertake physical challenges such as the American Birkebeiner, how much more important is this principle when we pursue spiritual challenges. God did not design us to run the great race of faith alone. It is a team sport.

True friendship between Christians means providing mutual spiritual support. It means cheering each other on through the ups and downs of life, reminding each other of God's goodness and his promises. Remember, both friends are runners. Neither has arrived at the finish line. Be careful, though, not to share Bible verses or principles glibly, lest your friend feel you are condescending.

Rather, I know that I am cheered on spiritually and emotionally when my friend says, "I have confidence in God and I have confidence in you." She reminds me that God has proven faithful in the past. She does not hold out empty promises such as "Everything will turn out fine. You'll see." Instead, her carefully chosen words focus on God's character and his work in my life.

Encouragement through Words of Truth

I need encouragement most when I am discouraged, when I am feeling defeated or hopeless, or when I am just plain tired. The apostle Paul wrote, "For our struggle is not against flesh and blood, but against the rulers, against the authorities, against the powers of this dark world and against the spiritual forces of evil in the heavenly realms" (Eph. 6:12). We are engaged in a cosmic battle, and it isn't easy. Sometimes we grow weary. The opposing forces overwhelm us. We are tempted to give in and take the path of least resistance. We need encouragement to persevere on the path that God has laid out for us.

This path is not always clear to us. Everywhere we turn we hear contradictory messages. A friend of mine is worried about her teenage daughter. She related to me advice she received from three different people. One said, "As long as she's not on drugs or pregnant, turn a blind eye to everything. You don't want to know." Another said, "She's going to try all those things anyway. Just be her friend so that she feels comfortable enough to tell you when she's in trouble." A third emphasized, "We kept our daughters on a tight leash. We wanted to know everything, and we did anything to find out what they were up to. We listened in on telephone conversations, went through dresser drawers, whatever it took to stay one step ahead of them."

Whose advice should she follow? At vulnerable times such as these, we readily slip into adopting prevalent attitudes and corresponding behaviors, regardless of whether they are based on the truth.

That is why we need a friend who will gently remind us of what is true. This is an important part of encouragement. Hebrews 3:13 tells us, "But encourage one another daily, as long as it is called Today, so that none of you may be hardened by sin's deceitfulness." Daily we need the kind of encouragement that points us toward the truth. Otherwise we will find that we have swallowed the lies the world around us serves up constantly. We must be that kind of friend as well: one who lovingly speaks the truth.

But how do we speak the truth without becoming preachy? We know that a true friend listens without trying to solve her friend's problem. And how do we know what the truth is or which particular truth applies to our friend's situation?

This calls for wisdom. There is no easy formula for attaining wisdom. The Bible tells us, however, that God is the source of all wisdom and that he gladly and generously gives it to those who ask him (James 1:5). If we would encourage our friend, we must seek God and his wisdom with all diligence. We must try to learn God's mind (insofar as we are able) so that when asked, we can direct our friend in his ways.

God has revealed himself and given us his truth both in his written Word, the Bible, and in the person of his Son, Jesus Christ. If we want to be wise, we will offer ourselves completely to Jesus Christ and we will submit our lives to his Word. Wisdom comes when we try to find out what pleases him, and we do it (Prov. 15:33; Eccles. 2:26). This is not an easy process. It involves discipline, perseverance, and struggle. We fail often. Yet, even our failures provide material for wisdom if we learn from them.

Only in this context can we encourage our friend in the truth. We must acknowledge that we too are seekers. We too struggle and fail. Any verbal encouragement that does not come from an attitude of humility is not encouragement at all, nor is it true friendship. Condescension discourages. When someone approaches me with an attitude that says, "I know all the answers. Here's what you should do," I feel like a lower life form. That does not encourage me.

Here are some guidelines we all can follow to help us become a real encouragement to others.

Tell Our Friend What We Are Learning

A true friend encourages by telling her friend what she is learning. As we seek to know God and apply his truth to our life, each day provides opportunities for growth. By talking about what God is teaching us, we encourage our friend to listen for God's lessons in her life.

Rarely do Kathy F. and I talk that she does not bring up a Bible verse she read that day. She loves Jesus so deeply and so genuinely desires to please him, that she frequently refers to him in conversation. This encourages me greatly. As I inwardly digest the nuggets she shares, my spirit is nourished. Her devotion spurs me to seek God with singlemindedness. She makes me long for a closer walk with God simply by sharing what God is teaching her.

Tell your friend what God is teaching you in the laboratory of real life. God teaches us through our successes and our failures. We encourage our friend when we disclose honestly the lessons we are learning in our struggles and in our triumphs.

In fact, I find that I understand those lessons only as I reflect on them with a friend. Only when I stop to mull over my current situations do I open myself to the possibility of enlightenment and growth. I consider how I am reacting and why. I contemplate how I got to this place and what God may be teaching me. When do I take the time to ponder these larger questions? When I pour out my heart to my true friend.

Point Our Friend to Jesus

Jesus is by far the best friend any of us can ever have. He loves us with a love that is pure. He always has our best interest in mind. His friendship changes us such that we become better—less selfish, more loving, wiser, and more mature. Yet, even when we fail him, he is not disillusioned. He forgives us and helps us to start over again. Who could ask for more in a friend?

I am encouraged by friends who gently direct me to Jesus when I am distraught. Just last week I quarreled with a family member and behaved abominably. The relationship in shambles, I felt guilty, despondent, and fearful that I had caused irreparable damage.

Then Martha stopped by. When I confessed to her my wrongdoing, Martha declared God's forgiveness, quoting 1 John 1:9. This was no new revelation for me, yet her assurance of God's forgiveness helped me feel forgiven. I admitted my sense of futility and fear for the future. Martha recalled several specific ways God had worked in my family relationships in the past. As we prayed together, my despair ebbed away. In its place, hope flowed through me. I felt as if I had been seriously ill and suddenly the fever had broken.

Of course, Martha was right. God mended the broken places in my troubled relationship, and it healed stronger than ever. Yet, part of the healing process happened in my heart as Martha ministered to me, pointing me to Jesus, reminding me of his faithfulness. In my hour of darkness, I needed the light that only Jesus brings. Martha took my hand and led me into the light.

Encouragement through Deeds of Thoughtfulness

A true friend cheers her friend on with more than words. Small deeds of kindness speak volumes, and they, too, produce a mighty effect in encouraging friends. These acts often take no more than a few minutes, but they can make a huge difference in our friend's life.

A young collegian from Wisconsin shared with me how her friends encouraged her with deeds of thoughtfulness:

"I had a term paper to write in one weekend. Yes, I procrastinate. I was extremely depressed because it seemed an impossible task.

"One friend filled a picnic basket full of treats. Each half hour she had an envelope with a fun note such as 'Walk around the library and stop at the drinking fountain for some cool refreshment.' Or 'Here's some money for a cup of coffee—take a break—you deserve it.' My sister came to the library and sat and read books and wrote letters, just to keep me company. Two other friends surprised me by taking me for lunch; another friend picked me up and treated me to pizza for dinner.

"The paper was written and I thoroughly enjoyed the surprise encouragement. I was a fairly new Christian, and this definitely showed me a giving love."

Small deeds of kindness, especially during a time of discouragement, demonstrate our love and point our friend to Jesus, the source of our love.

Encouragement through Prayer

Perhaps the most important way we can encourage a friend is by praying for her. Certainly nothing else we do for her brings the benefits of our efforts in prayer on her behalf. Too often we regard prayer as a mere postscript in the letter of our love for our friend. Make no mistake about it: Persistent, consistent prayer for a friend takes commitment, discipline, and thoughtfulness. It is hard work!

In his classic work entitled *Prayer*, Norwegian theologian O. Hallesby wrote:

> The most important work we have to do is that which must be done on our knees alone with God, away from the bustle of the world and the plaudits of men. . . . If the labor of prayer does not precede, as well as accompany, all of our work in the kingdom, it will become nothing but a work of man, more or less capably done and with more or less effort and agitation as the case may be, but resulting in nothing but weariness both to ourselves and to others.
>
> The work of praying is prerequisite to all other work in the kingdom of God, for the simple reason that it is by prayer that we couple the powers of heaven to our helplessness, the powers which can turn water into wine and remove mountains in our own life and in the lives of others, the powers which can awaken those who sleep in sin and raise up the dead, the powers which can capture strongholds and make the impossible possible.[1]

Instead of taking an approach that says, "When all else fails, pray," we need to practice this approach: "Before anything is attempted, pray." In so doing, we can greatly encourage our friend.

Nothing heartens me more than the assurance that a friend is praying for me. That tells me I am on her mind and in her heart. It tells me she cares about me enough to remember me regularly as she brings her requests to God.

Beyond that, however, I am encouraged because I know that ultimately only God can help me. And God has chosen to work through the vehicle of prayer. In some mysterious way, prayer unlocks the door to God's power and presence in our circumstances. I know that my friends' prayers accomplish more in my life than any other boon.

When a friend says, "I've been praying about such and such a matter in your life. How's it going?" her words lift my spirits. When I am bound up with anxiety, nothing loosens those bonds like the words "I am praying for you." These assurances of prayerfulness remind me that God is at work in my present situation. I need not fear. My confidence lies not in my abilities, nor in the abilities of my friends. My confidence is rooted in the nature and character of God himself. This knowledge strengthens me and enables me to press onward.

In the final analysis, God is the true encourager, even as he is the one true friend who is closer than a brother. He has given us his Holy Spirit to dwell in us as our counselor: "one called alongside to help." This is a good definition of encouragement.

The Holy Spirit gives us joy to encourage our hearts. He encourages us with his presence. He encourages us by leading us into all truth, guiding us, teaching us, and showing us how to apply God's Word to our lives. He encourages us by working in our lives, revealing answers to prayer and other blessings that come from God's hands. Finally, he encourages us by interceding for us in prayer, especially when we are too discouraged or overwrought to articulate our needs to God.

He who is our great encourager and friend calls us to engage in his ministry of encouragement and friendship. We must show true friendship by encouraging one another daily, committing the results to God.

Questions for Personal Reflection

1. Read again Hebrews 3:13. How does encouragement keep us from becoming hardened by sin's deceitfulness?

2. Where do your strengths lie in terms of encouraging your friends? Where is there room for growth?

3. Read the Book of Ruth. How was Ruth an encouragement to her discouraged friend and mother-in-law, Naomi?

*True friendship
is never serene.*

Marie De Sevigne

Going against the Grain

8

arbara and I have been friends for more than two decades," Sarah told me. "We got to know each other in high school, and somehow the friendship stuck. We enjoy the same movies and TV shows. If I discover a wonderful book, I know she will love it too. And we've been friends for so long that we share many memories—we have so much history together.

"But we have one huge difference. I am an evangelical Christian, and Barbara is Jewish. We have always spoken freely about our faiths with one another, but only on a comparative basis. We are not able to commune in these deeper matters.

"A few years ago I became very concerned about Barbara's eternal destiny. I felt guilty for being remiss in explaining the gospel message to her. I invited her over for dinner and had a frank discussion with her about Jesus' claims as the Messiah. Barbara listened politely, admitting that she did not read the Bible. I challenged her to try it, and that was the end of the discussion.

"She seems to respect my opinions and my faith, but she doesn't feel any need to change her beliefs at this point. And I don't feel I should pressure her. I'm glad I told her what I believe and what I wish for her. Now the ball is in her court.

"She and her husband include our family in some of their religious traditions. Last spring we were guests at their Passover seder—an incredible experience. Sometimes I feel a bit like the token Christian at their gatherings, but I continue to learn about her heritage and perspective. Recently the two of us toured the Holocaust Museum together. Barbara's mother is a Holocaust survivor, so this tour was a terribly moving, deeply personal experience for Barbara. It was very intimate to share those moments with her. I feel privileged that she allowed me to be a part of that experience with her.

"I don't know what lies ahead for Barbara in her faith journey. I hope that someday she finds the peace and joy I have found in my relationship with Jesus Christ. And the assurance of eternal life. But no matter what happens, I will always value our friendship, differences and all."

Once in a while we find a friend who seems to be cut from the same cloth we are. We think alike, react in similar fashion, enjoy the same activities, and share common beliefs. We feel as if we are "twin sisters who were separated at birth," to quote my fourteen-year-old friend, Isabel. This is a rare exception, however.

Usually friendships start out with commonality, but as we share more and more of ourselves with each other, we run up against differences. The better we get to know someone, the more disparities we are likely to find. This should come as no big surprise. Each of us is a unique individual. No one duplicates me in genetic makeup and personal history. Of course others see the world a bit differently than I do. It makes perfect sense.

Why then do I feel threatened by dissimilar opinion, personality, or taste? Perhaps I struggle with this more than most. But even a glance at the daily newspaper shows me that many of us are uncomfortable with differences. Are not the strains between races, ethnic groups, and cultures the result of people uncomfortable with differences? Rifts occur in families as the younger generation adopts views, dress, or lifestyles that are different from those of their parents. Friendships also harden and crack under the stress of disagreement.

How we respond to our disparities determines the depth and quality of our friendships. Our response to this challenge is critical if we want to grow both individually and in our friendships.

There are many ways of responding to differences. Some are healthy and lead to growth; others are destructive. Some are active; others are passive. Our responses often depend on the issue or area of difference. Certain issues are "hot buttons" for each of us.

What are some of the ways we respond to differences, and how can we respond in a way that encourages growth?

Avoidance

As a people pleaser who has a strong aversion to conflict, I naturally avoid potentially controversial issues. This was evident in an incident in the early stages of my walking group friendships.

One crisp September morning, my walking group decided to shift course, departing from the bike path and heading down the main street of our town. Our destination: a wonderful eatery that serves pastries and coffee in addition to other gourmet delights.

As we walked down the main street (a course we had never before taken), we passed directly in front of the abortion clinic. A solitary woman paraded up and down the sidewalk in front of the clinic carrying a pro-life sign.

I have strong convictions about the sanctity of life and the importance of protecting unborn children. It grieves me that an abortion facility operates in the middle of my town. Typically, I try to encourage pro-life demonstrators and sidewalk counselors when I pass them in front of this clinic.

Not this day, however. On this occasion, I did not acknowledge her. No one in our walking group did. We almost brushed up against her, yet none of us greeted her or remarked about her.

Why this conspiracy of silence? I can only guess what the others were thinking. At this point, I did not know my new walking partners well. I knew they did not view life from my biblical framework. I chose silence over introducing a controversial subject into our fledgling friendships. I reacted to the possibility of conflict with my standard response—avoidance.

Avoidance is not always bad. When a friendship is young, it needs nurturing. This is not the best time to don the boxing gloves. My reason for my eye-averting reaction held merit, I believe. Why take on such an emotionally charged issue? There did not seem to be any reason to hash that one out in our walking group. My new friends and I seemed to be coming from entirely different places, with very different core beliefs. I had no expectation that they would embrace my ethical stance. Arguing about this volatile matter would do nothing to communicate to them the love of Jesus Christ.

We certainly do not want to argue about everything about which we disagree. At some point, we have to decide if an issue is important enough to become a focal point in a relationship. Many of our differences are in peripheral issues, not in issues central to us or our friendship. In such cases, a little bit of avoidance can be a good thing.

On the other hand, those of us inclined to avoid conflict rarely distinguish between peripheral and central issues. When differences surface in core issues, we avoid those with even more energy than the peripheral ones. And that response is destructive. It shortchanges the friendship as well as cheating us out of an opportunity to grow.

"Peace at all costs" leads to stunted growth. We grow when we are challenged to think things through and try to see things from a different perspective. That is not to say we will always drop our own viewpoint and adopt our friend's differing one. Often we become even more convinced of our original position. However, a thorough discussion of the various facets of the subject strengthens us. We grow through the process. We come to a better understanding of the issue, our friend, and ourself.

Why do most of us avoid dealing with differences? Insecurity and fear. We are not confident enough in who we are and what we believe. We fear that when challenged, our core beliefs will not stand up to scrutiny. Or we fear that we will be made to look stupid because we cannot adequately defend our position. We fear ridicule and rejection.

The Bible speaks to these fears. David wrote, "The LORD is my light and my salvation—whom shall I fear? The LORD is the stronghold of my life—of whom shall I be afraid?" (Ps. 27:1). Again, David wrote, "In God, whose word I praise, in God I trust; I will not be afraid. What can mortal man do to me?" (Ps. 56:4).

These verses assure us that our fears are groundless. If we are in league with the God of the universe, then we could not be more secure. We trust not in ourselves, our views, or our positions on various issues. We trust only in the God of the Bible. He does not need our defense. He is not threatened by mortal man's upheld fist. We rest with unshaken confidence in God.

When you think about it, avoidance makes very little sense. No matter how hard we try to avoid something, it usually keeps cropping up. Eventually we have to confront it. And in the meantime, avoiding it takes a lot of energy and causes much stress. Why not deal with it and be done with it?

While we never directly tackled the issue of abortion in my walking group, we did come to an implicit understanding of each other's positions as we got to know one another better. Differences surfaced one by one. Each was a test case: Will she still want to be my friend, even if she doesn't agree with me? With every affirmative came another layer of trust in the foundation of our friendships.

Now that our friendships are solidly established, I feel completely at ease voicing my opinions, even on matters where my views may diametrically oppose the views of my friends. We love each other regardless of widely disparate beliefs, and our commitment to one another allows us to talk about those issues without fear of reprisal in the relationship.

The Bible assures us in 1 John 4:18: "There is no fear in love. But perfect love drives out fear, because fear has to do with punishment. The one who fears is not made perfect in love."

True friendship makes avoidance unnecessary.

Parting Ways

Distancing ourselves from our friend because of an uncomfortable difference is the ultimate avoidance. Often we respond this way unconsciously. We deal with unresolved issues by not dealing with them.

Lisa and Valerie work at the same office and have children the same ages. For several years now they have eaten lunch together daily and swapped stories about the trials and tribulations of parenting teenagers.

Valerie is a super-mom type with very strong opinions about parenting. Lisa takes a much more laid-back approach to parenting. She loves her children, but she does not make them the focus of her life as does Valerie. Valerie made a special effort to influence Lisa to be more like her, but Lisa did not "get with the program."

Finally, when problems spiraled out of control with one of Lisa's children, Valerie had had it. She felt frustrated that all her attempts to remedy the situation had failed. If only Lisa had heeded her advice, Lisa's children wouldn't be in such bad shape. She began to distance herself from Lisa. She arranged other commitments during lunch hour. Eventually their paths diverged.

Valerie decided she could not live with their differences in parenting styles. For her, this was a central issue. Continuing the friendship, in her mind, constituted approval of Lisa's methods.

As you can well imagine, Lisa felt bewildered and betrayed by Valerie's rejection. "Just when I'm in trouble, she's abandoning ship!" she complained to me. Lisa's bewilderment turned to bitterness as she realized that Valerie essentially demanded conformity. "In order to be my friend, you need to do things my way," was Valerie's underlying message.

This unfortunate situation illustrates several healthy reasons for parting ways as well as unhealthy reasons for ending a friendship.

Sometimes it is necessary to sever a friendship because of irreconcilable differences on core issues. If your friend's values are antithetical to your own, that gap may be too great to bridge. More importantly, you risk compromising your own principles by continued association with this friend. We tend to assume the qualities of those with whom we spend time. We see this phenomenon with teenagers, which is why we pray that our adolescent children will choose their friends wisely. As adults, we are less easily influenced, but we are influenced nonetheless.

This reason does not apply to Valerie, however. Valerie does not run the risk of being influenced by Lisa's relaxed approach to child-rearing. Lisa, on the other hand, had legitimate reason for parting company with Valerie, once it was evident that Valerie was out to change her. Valerie's inflexibility and her unwillingness to accept Lisa or to work through their differences prohibited friendship.

Sometimes different parenting styles or philosophies force a shift in a friendship because the friendship is having an adverse effect on our children. This is particularly true when our children are small. If I want to train my children to choose their friends carefully as they enter puberty and adolescence, then I will not throw them in with rebellious children when they are young—even if the children's mother happens to be my close friend.

That does not mean I have to sacrifice the friendship altogether. This dilemma calls for creativity and diplomacy. I can initiate "moms only" outings. Sometimes these problems resolve themselves over time, if in the meantime we can avoid alienating our friend without endangering our children.

What is a wrong reason for letting differences divide us? Often we simply prefer distancing ourselves or cutting off a friendship to the discomfort of dealing with our differences. We take the path of least resistance.

Most of the time, this is not a conscious decision. When we become uncomfortable in a friendship due to differences that arise, we begin to avoid that friend. Before we know what has happened, the friendship has fallen by the wayside.

Oh, well, we think, *that friendship just wasn't meant to be. We were too different.* We blame the dissolution on fate or God when our laziness alone is to blame.

The response of distancing or cutting off a friendship generally does not happen just once. Differences arise in the next friendship, and once again the response is distance. A pattern forms. The person who responds this way finds that she has few if any long-term friendships. Not only is she missing out on the blessings of deep, lifelong friendships, but she has turned away from opportunities for personal growth.

Criticism

Another more active response to differences is criticism. Implicit in Valerie's response to Lisa was an attitude of criticism. Everything she said and did intimated disapproval. I cannot think of circumstances in which this is a laudable response for a friend. Even when a friend is involved in grave, deliberate sin, a critical attitude does nothing to restore her to the straight and narrow.

That does not mean we should approve of anything and everything our friend does or says. We may continue to disagree strongly, believing beyond a shadow of a doubt that we are right. In fact, there is something wrong if we do not have any strong convictions. And we have every right to speak directly to these issues with our friend, endeavoring to persuade her of our views.

Criticism comes into play when we do not respect our friend's ultimate right to make her own decision. We condemn our friend when her choices do not correspond to ours. In criticizing we say, "If you do not agree with me, I will withdraw my support of you." Such an attitude tears down rather than builds up. It erects roadblocks in the friendship.

When our choices provoke condemning words or looks from our friend, we get the feeling that we do not live up to her standards. This impedes the progress of the friendship. We become cautious about what we tell her, knowing her tendency to judge. At this point, the friendship cannot go any deeper. Our friend's judgmental manner has had a chilling effect on our friendship. We drift apart.

A critical attitude all too readily manifests itself in speaking ill of someone. When we are faced with differences in a friendship and we are uncomfortable with these differences, what do we often do? We pick up the phone and call a third person to "get her perspective." Naturally, the person we call is one whom we know will see things our way. This validates our position and gives us a feeling of power. As despicable as this is, most of us behave this way at one time or another.

God roundly condemns this behavior. In Ephesians 4:29–32 we read,

> Do not let any unwholesome talk come out of your mouths, but only what is helpful for building others up according to their needs, that it may benefit those who listen. And do not grieve the Holy Spirit of God, with whom you were sealed for the day of redemption. Get rid of all bitterness, rage and anger, brawling and slander, along with every form of malice. Be kind and compassionate to one another, forgiving each other, just as in Christ God forgave you.

Clearly criticism and slander do not fit in with God's plan for us.

An Agenda for Change

Closely linked to criticism is the response of the agenda setter. This is the response of the friend who says to herself, *Clearly, she's missing the boat. I know what she needs to do to be on the right track. If I can just get her to this event, or hook her up with this person, or show her the benefits of my way of doing things, she will change her mind.* This friend has a wonderful plan for our life, and she sets herself to the task of implementing it, without our invitation or approval. Depending on her personality and ours, she either schemes or steamrolls.

She is uncomfortable with the difference between the two of us. Perhaps she has good reason to be uncomfortable. Perhaps she sees us doing things that are destructive to ourself and others. She wants what's best for us, and she is certain she knows what it is.

We might find ourself in the position of the agenda setter if we feel our friend would benefit from making changes in her life. It could be issues of parenting techniques, lifestyle, or current political hot topics, or it could be core issues of belief. We are coming from different positions, and we firmly believe we have truth on our side.

Here the question is not who is right and who is wrong. The focus of this discussion is our approach to this difference. Having an agenda involves behaving in ways that are less than direct and honest in order to achieve our goals for our friend.

Let me illustrate with an example given me by Melanie. For a brief interval several years ago, she tried her hand at having her own business. She became a consultant with a company that sells its product line by having its consultants convince friends to host consultations in their homes. Friends sell to friends who sell to friends. Recently, Melanie divulged how her business agenda caused her anguish:

"When I was a consultant, I had to approach people with the attitude, 'I'm so wonderful and I can help you to succeed too. Just agree to host one of my consultations.' I always had to have an agenda. I felt so uncomfortable with this that I became physically ill."

Melanie continued, "What especially sickened me was that I was hearing the same sort of message from the church. I was feeling pressure to have a soul-winning agenda for my friendships. But if I have an agenda, my friends won't feel safe with me."

Have you ever been invited to what you thought was a social event only to discover upon arrival that you were the unwitting target of a sales pitch? You have legitimate cause for feeling a bit resentful. You were deceived. We evoke the same feelings in our unbelieving friend when we invite her to gatherings where we plan to "sneak in the gospel message." In our desire to see our friend embrace our cherished beliefs, we employ methods that are far from Christian.

Jesus never misled any would-be followers. Far from it. He was so brutally honest that he tended to discourage people from following him. When he invited people to follow him or to make a radical change in their lives, he did so with honesty and respect. He never schemed, trapped, manipulated, or pressured. He simply told the truth and gave the other person the liberty to make the choice.

Likewise, when we hold beliefs that are different from those of our friend, we must be honest about where we stand. True friendship requires that kind of honesty. But we cannot expect our friend to listen to our positions and respect them if we are not willing to give our friend the same respect. Our friend will never be honest with us if she feels that we do not accept her, differences and all, the way she is right now.

Acceptance

How then should we deal with unpleasant differences? The answer is so simple, yet so difficult! God calls us to accept one another. "Accept one another, then, just as Christ accepted you, in order to bring praise to God" (Rom. 15:7).

Christ did not wait until we had our theology right before accepting us. He did not hold out until our lives jibed with his standards. We had nothing going for us when he reached out in love to us. "But God demonstrates his own love for us in this: While we were still sinners, Christ died for us" (Rom. 5:8).

Our acceptance must be genuine, not a phony front that masks an attitude of "I'll pretend that I accept you until you adopt my ideas. Then I'll really be able to relax and accept you."

How do we go about communicating genuine acceptance? First, our attitude once again should be one of great humility. We are not God. We do not know everything. Not one of us has a corner on truth.

We do have the Bible, the truth of God revealed in the pages of Holy Scripture. There he has clearly disclosed to us what is necessary for our salvation. On the other hand, the Bible leaves us with many unanswered questions.

In Deuteronomy 29:29, Moses told the people of Israel, "The secret things belong to the LORD our God, but the things revealed belong to us and to our children forever, that we may follow all the words of this law." God is infinite in his wisdom and knowledge, and he has not chosen to reveal everything to us at this point. Some things remain a secret. We cannot presume to fathom God's eternal mysteries.

Because we are so limited, our interpretation of God's Word is fallible, as is the way we apply it. Certain matters of morality and truth cannot be argued if we accept the authority of Scripture. But many issues that come up in our day-to-day existence, Scripture does not address directly. We must remember that throughout the ages, devout men and women of God have differed widely in their understandings of how God's Word applied to their lives. This should give us a large dose of humility and grace.

Second, a true friend shows acceptance through respect. When our friend signals through her behavior that she is uncomfortable with where we are leading a conversation, we respect her wishes. We back off. When we have expressed our opinions, we respect her right to decide for herself whether to adopt them. We don't try to pressure or manipulate. That is not treating her with respect and dignity. Rather, we respect her enough to allow her the freedom to make her own decisions.

Acceptance does not mean we agree with where our friends stand on all issues. It means we love and respect them even when we disagree vehemently.

Honesty

Ultimately, true friends deal honestly with their differences. In fact, differences can be freely aired because of the climate of acceptance. When we know our friend accepts us no matter what, we have freedom to share who we are. Differences are no better or worse than similarities.

We can honestly voice our opinions and feelings when we know our friend is not out to change us. And we can accept her opinions when we know it is not our job to change her. God has not given us that responsibility. Each of us is responsible for herself. God gave every Christian his indwelling Holy Spirit as his agent of change in our lives. We are released from the pressure of convincing our friend of the truth of our position because we know that if our belief is true, then God will convince her of that.

There are times when true friendship calls us to intervene in our friend's life. While we accept our friend, her behavior may be unacceptable. That is the subject of the next chapter. This difference, too, must be handled with humility, respect, and honesty.

When we are honest about our differences and accept one another despite them, we reap generous benefits. We take our friendships to new levels of trust. There is no comparison between a friendship limited to areas of agreement and a friendship that encompasses everything, including differences. Ironically, positive change most often occurs in a friendship marked by acceptance and honesty. We cannot help but grow when we are planted in such fertile soil.

Questions for Personal Reflection

1. How do you respond to differences? How have these reactions affected your friendships?

2. Read Romans 15:7. How did Christ accept us? (See also Romans 5:8.) What implications does this have for our response to our friends when differences surface?

3. Reread the love chapter, 1 Corinthians 13. How do these qualities apply to dealing with differences in a friendship? In light of this, what changes might you need to make in the way you handle differences?

We love those who know the worst of us and don't turn their faces away.

Walker Percy

9 *Tough Love*

Norma and Beverly met nineteen years ago when their daughters attended the same preschool. Both Norma's daughter, Heather, and Beverly's daughter, Michelle, have similar temperaments: strong-willed, independent, and assertive. Beverly became a Christian early in her friendship with Norma, thanks in part to Norma's loving influence. Together they sought to grow in their faith and to apply the truths they learned to their everyday lives.

Neither Norma nor Beverly had a good relationship with her mother. More than anything else, they wanted to have godly relationships with their daughters. Like unbroken fillies, however, the girls bucked against any direction their mothers gave. As the girls entered their teen years, the mother-daughter dynamics grew increasingly complex.

Norma found that when she was too embroiled in a conflict and couldn't see what she was doing wrong, Beverly could. And Beverly relied on Norma to be her eyes where she had blind spots. By unspoken agreement, Norma and Beverly agreed to be accountable to one another, particularly in regard to their behavior toward their daughters.

Over the years, Norma learned that Beverly's mother was extremely critical of her. Beverly bore the scars of a child who had never received a parent's blessing. So when Beverly related a conversation she had had with Michelle, Norma detected the mother-daughter pattern repeating itself. She saw that Michelle was feeling as if she could never live up to her mother's standards.

Because of the two friends' enduring commitment to one another, Norma was able to tell Beverly what was happening, and Beverly welcomed her friend's words. She knew they were spoken out of love and concern. She knew Norma understood her and her situation intimately. And without reservation, she desired to do what was right in her relationship with her daughter. Certainly she did not want to repeat the painful mistakes her mother had made. Beverly asked Norma to keep praying for her and reminding her of what was true and what was really important.

As the months and years went by, these issues continued to crop up. Norma steadfastly but gently continued to remind Beverly simply to be quiet rather than speak a critical word. "Just walk quietly, graciously, with Michelle. Don't try to be controlling. We do that when we let our fears kick in," Norma would say.

As the girls went off to college, it became more important for the mothers to pray more and say less. Their honest friendship helped them to stay on track. When Michelle and her boyfriend went through a difficult breakup, Beverly was quietly supportive. She did not criticize or advise her daughter. Instead, she fasted and prayed for her. Michelle began to react differently to this more positive, laid-back mom. She relaxed and allowed the mother-daughter friendship to take root.

Norma and Beverly helped each other become better mothers by holding each other accountable. Often one or the other felt like giving up on her relationship with her feisty daughter, but her friend was there to cheer her on. Words of encouragement and truth and even correction kept them pointed in the right direction.

Such is the loving accountability of true friendship. When a true friend holds us accountable, we are strengthened to keep our commitments. The resolve that so quickly fades away when we are on our own is fortified in the presence of an encouraging, watchful friend.

Contemporary North American culture scoffs at accountability. Our society practically worships privacy, and we unwittingly embrace the philosophy of "What I do is my business, and what you do is your business." We may shake our heads and cluck disapprovingly at our friends' choices. We may whisper about them to other friends. But we would never consider going to them directly and telling them what we think. After all, that's their business!

My friend Noreene, who has lived all over the globe, tells me that other cultures take a much more in-your-face approach. They do not hesitate to confront a friend who they feel has taken a wrong turn. In the turbulent societies of developing nations, interference in someone else's life often is a matter of life and death.

When the stakes are spiritual or emotional, rather than physical, it is much easier to rationalize our reasons for not getting involved. If we see something amiss in our friend's life, we resist calling it to her attention. Who wants to be the bad guy? At the very least we risk making our friend uncomfortable, and we don't like to do that. In the worst case, we risk losing the friendship. We certainly don't want that. So we keep our mouths shut.

This kind of isolationism does not promote true friendship. True friends hold one another accountable. I am willing to risk discomfort, even rejection if necessary, because I am committed to my friend's welfare. If she is engaged in dangerous or destructive behavior, I must intervene. Her well-being is paramount.

Components of Accountability

Commitment

Accountability requires commitment to the friendship and commitment to the friend. Accountability isn't easy. It takes us into areas of the relationship that are scary and unpleasant.

Most of us have the erroneous idea that friendship means only fun and good times. When a friendship moves beyond the comfort zone out into regions of insecurity, we often are tempted to "check out." *This is too stressful. I don't need this,* we say to ourselves.

The truth is that we do need this. We need friends who are committed to us enough to watch for red flags in our lives. We need friends who are committed to us enough to say the hard things that mere acquaintances will never say. We need friends who are committed to us enough to see us through our struggles. Such friends can make the difference in our lives between life and death, hope and despair, progress and backsliding.

Eloise and Jeannette sing together in their church choir. Both have beautiful voices and were music majors in college. The arching soprano voice of Eloise, and Jeannette's rich mezzo-soprano work well together in duets.

Several years ago, they were practicing their duet for the Christmas cantata when Eloise turned to Jeannette and said, "Every time I've heard you sing, I've wondered how you could have gotten a music degree when you have no voice control." Jeannette was stunned. "If you feel that way, how could you sing with me?" was her incredulous reply.

As Jeannette reflected on Eloise's thoughtless remark, she debated what to do. She was strongly tempted to avoid further encounters with her. Jeannette does not gravitate to difficult, potentially painful relationships, yet something inside her told her that she needed to be a friend to Eloise.

"I committed myself to be her friend no matter what," Jeannette told me. With a smile, she added, "I also decided not to sing with her anymore."

Several days later, Jeannette received an apologetic note from Eloise. Jeannette forgave her and moved ahead with the friendship. That incident was not the last bump in the road, however, and it was not the last time Jeannette wondered if she was out of her mind hanging on to this prickly, unpredictable friend.

"It was a very objective decision," she said to me. "I knew that this was going to be a difficult friendship. Either I was going to commit myself to it or walk away from it. I decided to commit myself to it."

Because of this commitment, Jeannette has been able to be honest with Eloise when Eloise makes other hurtful comments. She now knows that Eloise sabotages friendships because she feels herself unworthy of love. Because Jeannette refused to be run off, she broke through Eloise's self-erected barriers. Bolstered by Jeannette's true friendship, Eloise has grown in her ability to give and receive love.

Mutuality

Accountability in true friendship must be mutual. One-way accountability is not friendship—it's slavery. If we hold our friend accountable without submitting ourself to her in like manner, then we assume an unhealthy parental role. She is an adult, but we are treating her like a child. She is our equal, but we are behaving as if she were inferior.

The apostle Paul instructed the Ephesians to "submit to one another out of reverence for Christ" (Eph. 5:21). The attitude of mutual submission is integral to our relationships in the body of believers. Accountability means submitting ourself to another by being answerable to her for our conduct, duties, and attitudes. As members of Christ's body, we are called both to hold each other accountable and to be accountable to each other. Ultimately, it is Jesus Christ to whom we are answerable. In the meantime, we mutually submit to one another in accountability as befits his humble servants.

Practically speaking, this means that we do not ask our friend to keep us informed concerning her progress toward her goals without us telling her how well we are doing in achieving the goals we have set for ourself. (Notice that we are not setting goals for her; we set goals for ourself.)

Confession

Mutual accountability means that we confess our sins to our friend even as we hear her confession. As James wrote, "Therefore confess your sins to each other and pray for each other so that you may be healed" (James 5:16). Confession of sins constitutes an important part of accountability.

I have seen the power of mutual confession in my prayer partnership with Linda. When we get together, we cut to the chase, and usually this involves sharing our discoveries of sin in our own hearts. What has God been teaching me? What sinful attitudes underlie my current difficulties?

This is the stuff of our conversations. Her confession triggers a confession on my part. God uses these times to reveal to us new insights about ourselves and our relationships with God.

Then as we pray for each other, we perform for each other the priestly role of bringing our friend to God and giving our friend assurance of God's forgiveness. Nothing can compare with the sense of peace, cleansing, and wholeness that we experience after these times of confession and prayer. Just as the verse from James says, mutual confession and prayer result in healing. We need confession in our friendships so that we can become whole people who are being healed from the crippling effects of sin.

Teachability

I generally prefer praise to correction. Most people do. I would much rather hear someone tell me how wonderful I am than what I did wrong.

But I know that God is not pleased when I avoid correction. Furthermore, I lose by this attitude. "He who listens to a life-giving rebuke will be at home among the wise," says Proverbs 15:31. Proverbs 12:1 says, "Whoever loves discipline loves knowledge, but he who hates correction is stupid." Do I want to be foolish and stupid, or do I want to be knowledgeable and wise? The choice is mine. I make my choice by either avoiding or embracing correction.

Accountability works in friendship when there is a spirit of teachability—an attitude that says, "Lay it on me. I want to hear what you have to say, however painful, because I want to grow." We all have blind spots. Teachability recognizes that and asks the true friend to enlighten us. We are able to do this in the safety of a true friendship because we know beyond a shadow of a doubt that our true friend has our best interest at heart.

Mercy and Grace

Accountability does not mean that we have license to beat up our friend. And, of course, a true friend would not want to be harsh. When we love someone, we willingly extend grace.

I must extend grace to my friends because I know how much I need their grace. I am far from perfect myself. I mess up in small ways on a fairly regular basis, probably more frequently than I realize. And I occasionally make a whopper of a mistake. At such times, I thank God for true friends who show me mercy even as they hold me accountable.

First Peter 4:8 tells us, "Above all, love each other deeply, because love covers over a multitude of sins." True friendship does not hold a magnifying glass up to our failings. Rather, true friendship reflects the love of a merciful and gracious heavenly Father. As Psalm 103:10 puts it, "He does not treat us as our sins deserve or repay us according to our iniquities." We must demonstrate God's fatherly compassion when we come up against our friend's frailties.

As a result, there are many things we simply overlook. We give our friend slack, recognizing that God is at work in her life and she is in process even as we are. In the things we cannot overlook, we approach our friend with gentleness, believing the best about her.

A Case Study in Accountability

Unfortunately, the best is not always true. All of us have areas of weakness where sin can creep in and gain a foothold in our lives. We become blinded by our own evil desires, and we rationalize behavior in ourselves that we previously condemned in others. Before long, we are caught in sin's deadly tentacles. This is when the account-ability of true friendship can rescue us from the murky depths of sin and self-deceit. A true friend must call us out of danger. But the choice is ours. We may choose to follow her voice or we may choose to follow our own desires.

Such a situation arose in the friendship of Miriam and Alicia.[1] They were roommates and best friends all through college. After college, they found an apartment together. Alicia took a job as music director on the staff of a small but growing evangelical church. Miriam joined the church as well. Both became involved in the exciting ministry for young adult singles.

Several months into Alicia's new job on staff, Miriam noticed that Alicia frequently mentioned her conversations with Randall Graves, the youth and young adults minister. Randall was in his early thirties, a dynamic leader with a fun, outgoing personality. Randall was also married. His wife, Terri, stayed home to care for their three young children.

At first Alicia talked about their ministry-related discussions. Soon she and Randall were meeting for tennis on Saturday afternoons at Randall's indoor racquet club. Miriam did not say a word when Alicia revealed that she had decided to join the racquet club. Every time she watched Alicia bounce off to the club, tennis racquet in hand, a knot formed in Miriam's stomach. It wasn't just the tennis. Alicia revealed her feelings for Randall in the way she said his name, in the way she lunged for the telephone, in her whispered tones when he called.

After much prayer and careful thought, Miriam decided to say something. "Alicia, do you really think it's wise to be spending so much time with Randall? You see him at work, you see him at church and at young adults. Now you're seeing him during his time off, when he should be with his family."

"I'm not doing one thing wrong," Alicia flared. "So we both like tennis! He needs the exercise and so do I. We're just hitting a tennis ball back and forth, Miriam. There is absolutely nothing going on, and I am offended that you would even think such a thing."

Miriam dropped the subject. She continued to watch and pray. When Alicia's birthday rolled around in February, Alicia received a stylish tennis dress from Randall. Soon afterward, Randall began picking Alicia up for their tennis outings.

One Saturday afternoon, Miriam happened to be arriving home at the same time as Alicia and Randall. Instantaneously, she decided to confront them. Her pent-up emotions boiled dangerously close to the surface. Alicia and Randall turned from gazing into each other's eyes to see Miriam standing beside the car, glowering at them, arms folded across her chest.

"What's the matter, Miriam?" Randall asked in a friendly, innocent tone as he emerged from the car.

"You know very well what the matter is," Miriam fumed. "Randall, you have a wife and three children. Does Terri know that you play tennis with Alicia every Saturday?"

"I don't see what concern that is of yours, Miriam," Randall replied with forced steadiness.

"Miriam, what is your problem? Will you just leave us alone?" Alicia exploded and bolted into the house.

"Really, Miriam, there is nothing to worry about here," Randall reassured her in soothing tones.

Miriam turned and mounted the steps in silence. She knew otherwise. From that time on, Alicia grew distant and secretive. When Randall gave Alicia an expensive leather jacket, Miriam knew it was time to take the next step.

First, she went to the pastor of the church. He listened and assured her that he would look into the matter. Later, Miriam learned that when confronted by his boss, Randall painted a picture of a relational triangle, with Miriam as the jealous odd man out. He was able to convince the pastor that his behavior and intentions were above reproach. He made Miriam look petty and foolish.

By this time, Miriam and Alicia were functioning as polite roommates but no longer as close friends. Miriam learned from another member of the young adults group that Randall and Terri were seeing a marriage counselor. Alicia came and went with no explanation of her whereabouts, but Miriam saw telltale signs of foul play everywhere. She was tired of being the bad guy, but she didn't know how she could stand living in the midst of all this deceit. She considered moving, but that would mean a significant increase in rent, an expense Miriam could not afford. Despite her aversion to the whole situation, Miriam felt she should not simply cut off her friendship with Alicia. Her convictions told her that if ever Alicia needed a godly friend, it was now.

Finally, she went to the pastor again. Miriam hoped that this time he would believe her and do something to unmask the charade. Once again he promised to pursue the matter, acknowledging that he too had observed questionable dynamics between the two members of his staff. When confronted a second time by the pastor, Randall confessed that he had fallen in love with Alicia. He did not repent of it, nor did he admit to doing anything wrong. He resigned his position at the church, broke the news to his wife, and left town with Alicia, all within twenty-four hours.

Miriam was still reeling when the shock waves hit the Christian community—in the church, in the town, and in the church at large. For weeks Miriam heard about nothing but the scandal and the damage it had caused. Randall's wife was devastated, and his former friends and colleagues were outraged. Young people to whom Randall had ministered responded with anger and confusion. The once-thriving youth group evaporated. Miriam watched with dismay as sexual sin proliferated among the young adults. People seemed to have the attitude, "Well, he could do it. Why shouldn't I?"

Within a year, Randall's divorce was final, and he married Alicia. The ripple effect of their sin continues to this day.

Despite the fact that Miriam was vindicated, this outcome gave her no satisfaction. She grieved most of all for Alicia and for the friendship that they had shared and then lost. She hurt for Terri, left alone to raise three small children on her own. As angry as she was with Randall, Miriam lamented that the church lost such a dynamic leader. Finally, she was sickened that this sin besmirched the name of Jesus. She passed many sleepless nights replaying events in her mind, wondering if she could have handled things differently and so changed the outcome.

Clearly Miriam could not have stood by silently when she saw signs of danger followed by out-and-out sin. As Alicia's friend, it was Miriam's responsibility to confront Alicia. When direct confrontation with Alicia failed, her obligation continued, as a Christian as well as a friend.

In Matthew 18:15–17, we read Jesus' instruction concerning when and how we are to confront a fellow Christian:

> If your brother sins against you, go and show him his fault, just between the two of you. If he listens to you, you have won your brother over. But if he will not listen, take one or two others along, so that "every matter may be established by the testimony of two or three witnesses." If he refuses to listen to them, tell it to the church; and if he refuses to listen even to the church, treat him as you would a pagan or a tax collector.

These verses give us clear guidelines on how to handle a delicate, often sticky situation. One would think that Christians would be relieved to know exactly how to respond in a difficult relational matter. Unfortunately, the opposite is true. These principles are seldom obeyed in the Christian community, much to our detriment. Our concept of love has degenerated to a bland, safe niceness from the tough kind of love that Jesus prescribed—a love that risks everything for the well-being of the loved one.

Questions to Consider before Confronting

When should we embark on this risky course? Here are some questions we should ask when we are considering whether to confront a friend.

What Are the Facts?

When troublesome issues arise, emotions are likely to run high. Add to that bubbling cauldron the ingredient of rumor and we have a recipe for disaster. It is essential to take the time to sort out fact from fiction.

Does the Matter Pertain to Our Relationship?

If there has been a breach in our relationship due to some offense, it is our responsibility to go directly to our friend and try to resolve the matter. Sometimes that means asking, "Have I offended you in some way?" Other times it means saying, "I need to tell you that you hurt me."

The Bible urges us to keep short accounts with our friends. "Therefore, if you are offering your gift at the altar and there remember that your brother has something against you, leave your gift there in front of the altar. First go and be reconciled to your brother; then come and offer your gift" (Matt. 5:23–24). The point is not who offended whom. The key is to go and be reconciled.

God did not give us the liberty to hoard offenses with attitudes that say, "If she doesn't call me, I just won't call her.

Why should I bow and scrape? I didn't do anything wrong."
Nor did he tell us to distance ourselves from our friends
when they have offended us. God desires reconciliation.

Is Our Friend Deliberately Disobeying God?

We all sin. It is not our place to point out our friend's
each and every wrongdoing. On the other hand, we are
obligated to say something when our friend willfully
engages in continued wrong behavior. When Miriam saw
that her friend and roommate, Alicia, continued to par-
ticipate in a secretive, romantic relationship with a married man, Miriam had a moral obligation to speak up.

Is Our Friend Unknowingly Placing Herself in Danger?

When my daughter was two years old, she toddled out
into the street in front of our house, despite my stern
injunctions. She was willful, as most two-year-olds are,
determined to see what I would do if she defied me. Naturally, I raced after her and swept her up and out of harm's
way. At her tender age, she had no idea of the consequences
that would befall her if she played in the street.

Particularly if your friend is a new believer, she may not
understand the consequences of certain behaviors. Like my
daughter, she might unwittingly be putting herself in
harm's way. I am not saying that we should give our friend
a list of Christian do's and don'ts. Nothing could be further
from the gospel message. But if we detect true moral or spiritual danger, we must intervene out of our love for her.

Linda was a new Christian when we became friends.
Despite our disparity in background and spiritual matu-
rity, we both hungered for friendship. Each of us looked
forward to our time together as the highlight of the week.

One day Linda divulged something that raised a red flag
for me. Because she was young, new to the faith, and pure

in heart, she did not suspect that anything might be amiss when a married man from our church began to call her to talk about spiritual things. For several months, I listened and said nothing as she innocently referred to these telephone conversations.

Finally, one day I ventured, "Linda, do you really think he should be calling you? Shouldn't he be talking about these things with his wife?"

Linda's face registered sudden awareness. "You are right! Oh, my goodness!" Linda gasped. The next time he called, Linda informed him that she no longer welcomed his calls. Linda and I both felt immense relief. That man and his wife divorced several years later. I am so grateful that Linda heeded my warning and removed herself from a dangerous situation.

Is Our Friend's Behavior Harmful to the Body of Believers?

Our friend may be doing something that is not willful, deliberate sin, but it is sin that will have a ripple effect in the church. Gossip and slander are good examples. These are bad habits born of bad attitudes, and they poison others' attitudes. Relationships, reputations, even lives can be damaged or destroyed by such idle words. If such behaviors crop up in our friend on more than an occasional basis, we must go to her in love and confront her. As a friend, it is our responsibility to her. As a Christian, it is our responsibility to the Christian community.

What Is Our Motivation for Confronting Our Friend?

Is love for her the driving force in our urge to speak to her about our concern? Or is it a need to "set her straight" or "make her see things our way"? Perhaps we are reacting to something in our friend that we fear facing in ourself. Love is the only valid motivation. If our reason is not love, then we are not the person to do the confronting.

How to Proceed If Confrontation Is Necessary

If after considering these questions we determine that our love for God and for our friend compel us to confront her, here are some tips on how to proceed.

Pray

We should pray as we consider the above questions. Then we should pray some more before we speak to her, asking God to prepare her heart and ours, asking him to give us the right attitude and words, asking him for grace in communicating our loving intentions. Submit ourself to God to be used for his good purposes whatever the cost. Commit the outcome to his sovereign, loving hands. Continue to pray as we go to her. Pray as we speak and pray afterward.

Keep It Confidential

Proverbs 17:9 tells us, "He who covers over an offense promotes love, but whoever repeats the matter separates close friends." Most matters can be resolved if we go directly, and exclusively, to the other person involved. If our friend receives our message, we find ourselves feeling greatly relieved that we did not tell others. Then we have upheld our friend's honor in other people's eyes, something true friends should always do for one another.

If our friend does not receive our message, then we are compelled to speak about the matter with another Christian, according to Jesus' directive in Matthew 18. We must make sure that the other person we talk to is a strong Christian who also loves our friend and has her best interest at heart. If the two of us fail to reach her, we must take up the matter with a pastor or leader in our church. Others need not know until such time as the issue comes before the church, if our pastor indeed follows these steps.

Go in Humility and Love

It is of paramount importance that we convey in our attitude, demeanor, words, and body language that we come as a fellow sinner. An attitude of humility and love is the sweet, refreshing water that helps our friend swallow the bitter pill of confrontation. Without this, she will surely choke on it.

If possible, we should go to our friend in person. Some people do well with letters, but for others, letters are deadly. Words are cold things on a page. They do little to convey the spirit of love and genuine concern. The telephone is almost as bad. Experts tell us that body language is more important to communication than the words we use. Our face, our touch, our stance can convey that we truly speak in love in a way that our voice over a telephone line cannot.

Remember That Restoration Is the Goal

If our goal is to restore our friend to a right relationship with us, the Christian community, or Jesus Christ, we can rest assured that we are on the right track.

However, we do not have the power to ensure that this will be the result. We can only speak the truth in love and entrust the outcome to God. If our friend receives our words, we rejoice and give praise to God. If our friend refuses to listen, we must pursue the course that Jesus laid out in Matthew 18, always keeping before us the goal of restoration.

Accountability between true friends functions as an agent that prevents disease and promotes healing. It binds us to one another in a way that gives us stability. And it serves as a bridge over chasms created by sin. True friends hold one another accountable, and in so doing, they become to one another conduits of God's grace, truth, and love.

Questions for Personal Reflection

1. Describe a mutually accountable friendship in your life. What makes it work? If you do not have one, why do you think this is absent in your friendships?

2. Consider James 5:16. How can mutual confession bring healing?

3. Reread Jesus' words in Matthew 5:23–24 and Matthew 18:15–17. How do you see these principles applying to your friendships?

What became of the friends I had
With whom I was always so close
And loved so dearly?

Rutebeuf

10 The Sting of Disappointment

egina and Angie had been close friends for
years.[1] When Regina began to avoid Angie,
Angie rationalized that Regina was simply very
busy and didn't have time to call or get together.
She needs some space, Angie thought. Instead of badgering her with phone calls, she wrote her a loving note in a pretty thinking-of-you card. Regina did not acknowledge the card.

A few weeks later, they ran into each other at the shopping mall. Angie rushed to embrace Regina, but she seemed so uncomfortable that Angie stopped short. Regina was polite but cool. After a few moments of strained conversation, Regina hurried off, leaving Angie blinking back tears of hurt and confusion.

Angie could deny it no longer. Something had come between them. But what was it? Was it something she had said? She played and replayed mental videotapes of all her interactions with Regina, but she couldn't think of anything she had said or done that might have offended her dear friend.

Finally, Angie called Regina on the telephone and asked her point-blank. Regina refused to admit that anything was wrong. She was busy with other pursuits, she said, and she cut the conversation short.

Angie felt miserable. She knew Regina had not been too busy to go out to lunch with other friends. Had one of those friends turned Regina against her? Or had Regina grown tired of her and discarded her like a worn-out garment?

Angie made several more attempts to reestablish the friendship, but she was rebuffed every time. She had to admit that she couldn't force Regina to be friends with her. She couldn't even pry out of her a reason for the change. And she did not want to compel Regina to say the words she most feared: "I don't like you anymore. You're boring. You get on my nerves." It was bad enough being rejected by someone she thought loved her; she didn't want the rejection shoved in her face.

An Unfortunate Reality

Few things hurt us so deeply as rejection, betrayal, and disappointment, especially from someone we considered a true friend. Some are so wounded by these experiences that they find it difficult if not impossible ever to trust another person again. When we love deeply and give ourselves completely to a friend, we render our hearts vulnerable to great pain and injury.

Disappointment is inevitable for one reason: We can only have sinners for friends. Jesus is the only human being who has ever walked this earth without sin. Every other person operates with the handicap of a fallen, sinful nature. We all feel the pull of pride, selfishness, insecurity, fear . . . the list goes on. Because we give in to these urges on a regular basis, we cause hurt to others—and others hurt us. It is part and parcel of living in a fallen world.

God knows this about us, of course. He has addressed these issues in the Bible because he does not want our relationships to degenerate into alienation, hatred, and war.

Rather, he desires that our relationships mirror his character of righteousness and love.

Letting Go of the Little Things

First, he tells us to be forbearing with one another. Ephesians 4:2 reads, "Be completely humble and gentle; be patient, bearing with one another in love." Then in Colossians 3:13 we read, "Bear with each other and forgive whatever grievances you may have against one another. Forgive as the Lord forgave you." This theme recurs throughout Scripture. God bears with us, showing patience as we continually fail him. He asks that we demonstrate that same patience with one another.

Forbearance means that we are not easily offended, annoyed, or provoked. First Corinthians 13:5 expands on the qualities of love, saying that "It [love] is not rude, it is not self-seeking, it is not easily angered, it keeps no record of wrongs." To put it another way, we do not show the love of God by taking offense over little things, making mountains out of molehills, or readily reacting in anger.

Too many friendships are severed because we do not bear with each other in love. We allow little issues to assume monumental proportions. We cling to our grievances and allow them to drive a wedge between us. These attitudes reflect pettiness, not the largess of spirit befitting a child of God.

In the book *Breakfast with the Saints,* editor LaVonne Neff records the words of St. Martin of Braga:

> Those who are wise overlook many wrongs and often do not take them as such, for either they do not know about them or, if they do, they make fun of them and turn them into jokes. To pay no attention to injuries is a mark of magnanimity. The really great and noble soul listens to wrongs as securely as the larger wild animals hear the barking of small dogs.[2]

The Four A's of a Complete Apology

One of the chief reasons we must show forbearance in our friendships is that we need others to be forbearing with us. We all disappoint our friends from time to time. We cause hurt, most of the time quite unintentionally. Sometimes our sin causes these relational snafus. Other times a perfectly innocent remark will touch a raw nerve in our friend, a vestige of older hurts due to others' sins.

In either case, we always need to be sensitive to our friends and watchful of our words and actions. And recognizing that despite our vigilance we will err, we must wear humility like a garment. This is the only proper attire for a Christian.

When we err, there is nothing to do but humbly seek forgiveness. Easier said than done. Often our apologies are so flippant or shabby that they fall far short of restoring the relationship.

I learned about apologies in the arena of marriage. There I discovered that my quick, ready apologies just didn't do the trick. Like a small child, I believed that saying the magic words "I'm sorry" made everything better. But when I continued to make the same hurtful mistakes, my words rang hollow.

Over the years I have learned that a true apology consists of four components. Here are four things we can do to communicate to a true friend that we are genuinely sorry.

Admit Our Wrongdoing

When God calls us to repent, he asks us to agree with him about our sin. He wants us to see that our sin is sin. When our children commit some childish transgression, we do not desire their prolonged guilt and anguish, but we do want them to see that what they did was wrong.

Similarly, we need to name our wrongdoing to our friend. This is the part that gets stuck in our throat like a fishbone. We do not like to admit that we are wrong. Our minds so readily justify our actions that we most often truly believe we are in the right.

That is why we need to listen carefully and with an open, teachable mind to our friend when she comes to us and tells us that we have offended her. We must discern what we have done wrong. However blameless we may think we are, on closer examination we usually find that we have contributed in some way to the breakdown in the relationship. Then we must admit to her specifically what we did wrong.

Acknowledge Her Feelings

When Daniel realized that according to the prophecies the time had come for the end of the Babylonian captivity, he donned sackcloth and ashes and confessed his own sin and the sin of his people. His prayer of confession, recorded in Daniel 9:4–19, serves as a model of humble repentance. In this confession, he acknowledges God's rightful punishment of the Jews.

> Therefore the curses and sworn judgments written in the Law of Moses, the servant of God, have been poured out on us, because we have sinned against you. You have fulfilled the words spoken against us and against our rulers by bringing upon us great disaster. Under the whole heaven nothing has ever been done like what has been done to Jerusalem. Just as it is written in the Law of Moses, all this disaster has come upon us, yet we have not sought the favor of the LORD our God by turning from our sins and giving attention to your truth. The LORD did not hesitate to bring the disaster upon us, for the LORD our God is righteous in everything he does; yet we have not obeyed him.
>
> Daniel 9:11–14

Here Daniel basically says, "You were absolutely right to pour out on us these horrible woes. We deserve your wrath."

When apologizing, I have found it helpful to say, "I don't blame you for being angry with me. If I were you, I'd be angry too." Another way that I have acknowledged my wronged friend's feelings is to say, "I can see where my words really hurt you."

By acknowledging our friend's feelings, we demonstrate that we understand (or at least we are moving in that direction). We are on her side, not pulling against her by defending our own position.

Ask for Forgiveness

This should be followed by the words "Will you please forgive me?" When we ask for forgiveness, we assume a humble posture. We submit ourself to our friend.

This question also makes it clear that the responsibility for restoration now lies with the offended party. She can either extend or withhold forgiveness. The consequent reconciliation or alienation lies within her power.

Agree On a New Course

Biblical repentance always implies a change in direction. As difficult as it may be to say the words "I'm sorry," mere words are not enough. Words must be followed by action.

Think carefully about what factors led to the hurt or misunderstanding. What can we do differently from now on so that we don't commit the same offense? If we can come up with a plan that serves as a preventative measure, we make a strong statement about our sincere intention to change. We want our friend to know beyond a shadow of a doubt that we are sorry to have hurt her, sorry enough to take decisive measures to prevent another occurrence.

This four-stage process presupposes that we know what it is we have done to offend our friend. It hearkens back to the importance of accountability. If our friend does not come to us with her grievance, how are we to know that we have

offended her? Worse still, if she simply withdraws and refuses
to talk about it, we stand helpless, unable to make amends.

Disappointment and Forgiveness

Hurts come our way from time to time. The most difficult hurts, however, are those, like Angie's, that we simply
do not understand. When lack of resolution is layered on top
of lack of understanding, we are force-fed a sandwich of confusion that is hard to swallow and even harder to stomach.

These are not the bumps and bruises that can be over-
looked. We cannot patch a bandage over deep wounds that
place a friendship in mortal danger. Deep hurts require
attention, and at one point or another, forgiveness will be
the recommended treatment.

A year ago I sliced my finger on the lid of a can of cat
food. The moment it happened, I thought, *Oh, no. Now
I've done it.* Obviously I needed stitches. I spent the
evening at a medical facility submitting to one unpleasant
procedure after another. My wound needed cleansing and
sutures. Without these attentions, my wound would not
have healed properly. It easily could have become infected.
But because it received prompt and thorough care, my cut
mended nicely, leaving only a faint white scar.

Our friendship rifts need the cleansing of loving confrontation and the sutures of forgiveness. The passage of
time along with gentle lovingkindness is like exposure to
air and light. It aids the healing process.

Without forgiveness, the body of Christ becomes maimed
and disease-ridden. Forgiveness is essential to the health
and life of our relationships.

Jesus minced no words on the subject of forgiveness. He
told his disciples that if they withheld forgiveness from a
Christian brother or sister, they jeopardized their own rela-

tionships with God. God's forgiveness of us turns on the condition of our forgiveness of others.

Jesus told a very interesting parable on the subject of forgiveness recorded in Matthew 18:21–35. He told it by way of explanation after Peter asked him if he should forgive his brother seven times (a generous offer—Jewish law specified three). Jesus replied that he should forgive his brother seventy times seven. In other words, there should be no cap on our forgiveness.

Then Jesus told the story of the servant who owed his master a debt of millions of dollars. When his master demanded the money, he begged for mercy. The master forgave him and canceled his debt. The servant went his way. A second servant owed the first servant a day's wage, but the first servant refused his pleas. He threw the second servant in jail until he could pay his minimal debt. Word got around, and a group of fellow servants told the master what had happened.

"Then the master called the servant in. 'You wicked servant,' he said, 'I canceled all that debt of yours because you begged me to. Shouldn't you have had mercy on your fellow servant just as I had on you?'" (Matt. 18:32–33). He then had the unmerciful servant thrown in jail to be tortured. Jesus concluded the parable with these words: "This is how my heavenly Father will treat each of you unless you forgive your brother from your heart" (Matt. 18:35).

Our own sin against God is so great that Jesus compares it to a debt of millions of dollars. In contrast, the sins others commit against us are mere pocket change. Because God in his mercy canceled our great debt, we in turn must show mercy to those who owe us little debts. For God's children, forgiveness is not an option. It is fundamental.

We must forgive not only for God's sake but for our own sakes. What is the opposite of forgiveness? Harboring grudges, anger, resentment, bitterness, vengefulness. These dark attitudes do not spring from God. Rather, they waft up from the pit of hell like poisonous vapors. They penetrate into the depths of our souls, twisting our minds, weakening our bodies, and killing our spirits.

Lewis B. Smedes, author of several books on forgiveness, says, "When we forgive, we set a prisoner free and discover that that prisoner we set free is us."[3] Bitterness is a prison. Forgiveness is the key that unlocks the door and sets us free—free to love, free to live.

It is easy to forgive a friend who comes to us in love and humility, asking for our forgiveness. The difficulty comes in forgiving a friend who is not sorry for the wrong she has done or the hurt she has caused. Either she refuses to acknowledge she did anything wrong or she breaks off the relationship and will not allow reconciliation, as in the case of Regina and Angie. One woman told me about how her husband left her and moved in with her best friend. Are we really expected to forgive under these circumstances?

The answer is yes. Francis A. Schaeffer wrote, "We are to have a forgiving spirit even before the other person expresses regret for wrong. The Lord's Prayer does not suggest that when the other person is sorry, then we are to show a oneness by having a forgiving spirit. Rather, we are called upon to have a forgiving spirit without the other person having made the first step. We may still say that this individual is wrong, but in the midst of saying that person is wrong, we must be forgiving."[4]

Smedes, in his excellent new book entitled *The Art of Forgiving: When You Need to Forgive and Don't Know How*, points out that forgiveness is not the same thing as excusing the wrong. Nor is forgiving tolerance. He writes, "Nor does forgiving a person mean that we invite him to get close enough to hurt us again. When we forgive someone who is not sorry for what he has done, we do not forget, and we do not intend to let it happen again."[5]

The woman who lost her husband to her "best friend" will never forget that wrong. No matter how fully she forgives her friend, she will never be close to her again. We cannot be restored to friendship with one who refuses to be sorry for the hurt she has caused us. Smedes puts it this way: "When we forgive someone who does not say he's sorry, we are not issuing him a welcome back to the relationship we had before; if he wants to come back he must come in sorrow. To *give* forgiveness requires nothing but a desire to be free of our resentment. To *receive* forgiveness requires sorrow for what we did to give someone reason to be resentful."[6]

Some Thoughts on Forgiveness

Many volumes have been written on the subject of forgiveness. Its theme is woven through the pages of some of the world's greatest literature. I think of such works as *The Brothers Karamazov* by Fyodor Dostoyevsky and *Les Miserables* by Victor Hugo.

Yet, forgiveness is a great mystery, for it emanates from God himself. Alexander Pope wrote, "To err is human, to forgive divine." We can analyze and categorize the ways in which we err, but forgiveness defies analysis. Forgiveness is a grace that comes from God alone. To try to reduce it to "six easy steps" would be presumptuousness bordering on hubris. Forgiveness cannot be fathomed, for it lies at the heart of the greatest mystery in the universe—God's acceptance of us through his Son's death on the cross.

Philip Yancey calls forgiveness "what may seem like the most unnatural act a person can perform."[7] Yet, God commands us to forgive. He expects us to do it. And the good news is that he enables us to do it.

As I consider the mystery of forgiveness and how to apply it to disappointments in friendship, I offer the following reflections.

Forgiveness Is a Decision

God never commanded us to do something that was out of our control. Obedience to him is not a matter of feeling a certain way. It is a matter of the will. Most of the time, our hearts are not transformed immediately. The decision to forgive our friend is not usually a once-and-for-all decision. We must continue to forgive even after our initial decision, because we will be tempted to lapse back into our resentment. Memories of the hurt will stir up old emotions, and we will find that we must decide again and again to forgive.

Every time resentment and bitterness resurface, we must let go of them. No matter how much we want to hang on to our rage, we must open our hands and let it fly away. This requires submitting our wills to God and trusting him to sort out issues of justice, punishment, and reward.

Forgiveness Means Committing Justice to God

When we have been deeply wounded, our natural desire is to punish the offender in some way. We do this by shutting her out, by turning others against her, by hurling sarcastic remarks at her, and countless other hurtful behaviors. If we are to forgive—for our own sake if not for our friend's—we must allow justice to rest in the hands of God. He alone knows all the facts. He knows our hurt. He knows every in and out of the situation. And he is the righteous judge before whom we all will one day stand and give an account for our deeds.

Forgiveness Means Blessing Not Cursing the Offender

God calls us to a radical kind of love with which we bless those who persecute us. This goes a step beyond giving up our own right to mete out justice. This pushes us to the limit, requiring that we actually wish the best for the person who offended us. Instead of desiring or delighting in her downfall, we want the very best for her.

Clearly, this requires the work of God in our hearts. We must seek him earnestly, asking him to give us his grace. Then we must do our part by actively blessing the person. Pray for God's best for her. Say nice things about her. Say kind things to her if she will allow it. Do things to honor, encourage, and bless her as opportunities present themselves.

Relinquishment

When we experience disappointment in our friendships, we must guard against resentment, for resentment is backward looking. If I try to drive a car forward while I continue to look over my shoulder, I cannot stay on the road. I veer off. The only direction I can drive while looking over my shoulder is in reverse (and I'm not too great at that either!). Forgiveness looks forward, and it enables us to go forward with our lives, if not with that particular relationship.

No matter what we do to restore our relationships, we cannot guarantee happy endings. We may give forgiveness, but if it is not received, we cannot be reconciled. There is nothing left but to relinquish that friendship, leaving the outcome to God. We do not close the door on the friendship. In fact, we leave it propped open in case she should change her mind and desire reconciliation. But in the meantime, we move on to new friendships. The experience leaves us sadder but wiser.

Healing takes time. These hurts leave us feeling ravaged. Sin always leaves scars, but God is in the business of healing wounded souls.

"The great secret: To hold on, let go. Nothing is solid. Everything moves. Except love—hold on to love. Do what love requires."[8]

Questions for Personal Reflection

1. Have you been disappointed in a friendship? What are your thoughts and feelings about that situation today?

2. Read Ephesians 4:2. What are some current issues in your friendships about which you need to "bear with [your friend] in love"?

3. What does "forgiving one another as Christ forgave you" mean in your experience?

*The best mirror
is an old friend.*

George Herbert

11 *The Sands of Time*

E llen's wedding was picture-perfect. As she glided down the aisle, her olive skin and jet-black hair a sharp contrast to her gossamer gown of white, I recalled that first time I saw her in Spanish class. Scenes from our friendship in junior high and high school flashed before my eyes. Laughing together—that is how I would always remember our friendship. A lump formed in my throat and tears stung the corners of my eyes. How would her marriage change our friendship? Things would never be the same. I knew that. But could our friendship endure?

Three years later, I was the one walking down the aisle, and Ellen was sitting in the pew. We had seen each other only once or twice in the intervening years. Now I was further straining the limits of our friendship. My marriage would take me one thousand miles away.

Not long after I moved, Ellen also moved out of the area. When I made it home to visit my family, Ellen was never there. Every year I sent Ellen a Christmas card. Sometimes I heard from her, and sometimes I didn't. Then one year my Christmas card came back to me with no forwarding address. I did not hear from her for many years, and I grieved the loss of this precious friendship.

Several years ago, I discovered that Ellen had moved back to our hometown. I contacted her while visiting relatives, and we talked for hours. We had both changed, yet we still seemed to connect. Once again, we tearfully bid each other good-bye. With one thousand miles between us and a shared weakness in the letter-writing department, Ellen and I face high hurdles in maintaining our friendship.

Kinds of Transitions

Transitions are difficult for all of us, but for friendships they can be deadly. Friendships form through proximity and affinity. When one of those factors changes, the friendship is in jeopardy.

Some transitions are changes that take place from the outside in. In other words, our outward circumstances change, and this causes a change within us or the relationship. Other changes are from the inside out. We change internally, and this affects our outward circumstances.

A Change in Location

A change in location is a dramatic, obvious, and stressful transition for a friendship. Some women have no problem leaving their friendships behind when they move. They live 100 percent in the present. Others see true friendship as a lifelong commitment. They expend tremendous effort maintaining friendships despite many obstacles. Most of us fall somewhere in between these two extremes.

Problems arise when two friends are opposites in this respect. The difference never surfaces until the transition. Then the committed friend ends up feeling abandoned, and the free-spirited friend feels guilty and burdened by the other's demands.

Heidi moved to the United States from Germany when her husband, an American serviceman, took early retirement and found a civilian job in the Washington, D.C., area. She found it difficult to adjust to the fast-paced American lifestyle, especially when it came to friendships. Everyone always seemed so busy! How she longed for the lazy afternoons she enjoyed with friends in Germany, drinking coffee and sharing their latest parenting tribulations.

Feeling a desperate need for friendship, Heidi joined a women's Bible study. Heidi was delighted when the leader paired her with a younger woman named Celia as a prayer partner. Heidi and Celia hit it off from the start. Heidi saw this friendship as the answer to her prayers. Heidi and Celia met or spoke on the telephone every week for two years. They shared all their concerns with one another, as well as their joys.

One day Celia broke the news that her family was moving to Florida. They would be staying with relatives while they hunted for a house. Celia promised to send her address once they knew for sure where they would live.

With a heavy heart, Heidi said good-bye to her cherished friend. Weeks passed without a word from Celia. Weeks turned into months. Still no letter, not even a change-of-address postcard. No one else at church had Celia's new address. Heidi had no way of tracking her down. Celia never wrote, and Heidi's heart was broken.

"I thought she was my friend. We had shared so deeply. I just don't understand how she could simply drop our friendship," Heidi said with tears in her eyes.

Perhaps there was some unspoken reason why Celia did not want to continue her friendship with Heidi. I suspect, however, that she busied herself in her new life and put the past behind her. Her friendship with Heidi was fine for that season of her life. Now that she was in Florida, she needed new friends who were taking up all her allotted friendship time.

Transitions do not usually yield such an abrupt blow. Typically we make promises of undying faithfulness, followed by good efforts. These efforts become less regular until they dwindle to the yearly Christmas card. If one of us doesn't send Christmas cards, soon we lose contact altogether. So ends a true friendship.

When something stirs a memory of a lost friendship, we grieve that loss. For years, whenever I thought of Ellen, I felt a physical pain in my chest. I missed her. I wanted her back in my life. Our friendship was precious to me, and its loss caused me great sorrow.

Distance is not the only transition that poses a challenge to a true friendship.

A Change in Relationship Roles

A change in relationship roles happens gradually, incrementally, yet it deeply affects the dynamics of the friendship.

When Linda and I embarked on our friendship journey, she had recently committed her life to Christ. She was just out of high school, single, and working while pursuing an education. I was considerably older—twenty-three years old! I had completed my college education and was married. I had been a Christian for as long as I could remember. In those early years of our friendship, I served as a mentor to Linda, teaching her how to study the Bible and pray. Let me hasten to add that I received equally as much if not more from the relationship as she did. I desperately needed a significant friendship as well as Christian fellowship, and Linda provided both. Her fresh excitement and love for Christ ignited zeal within my spirit.

As the years passed, Linda matured in her understanding and her experience of the Christian life. The time came when our friendship outgrew the roles of mentor and student. We were peers in our Christian walk.

The age difference that seemed so marked when we first began to be friends dwindled with the years. She married and had children, and those experiences also helped to put us on a par. I was no longer the older, married woman counseling the young single. We were two old married women struggling with raising families!

For our friendship, these role changes were beneficial. They brought a sense of mutuality and shared experience. Our understanding of one another deepened.

A Change in Lifestyle

Sometimes, however, a change in lifestyle poses tremendous problems for a friendship. Such changes radically transform our lives. They cannot help but change the friendship. Marriage changes us. We no longer have the freedom to do what we want to do when we want to do it. Candy told about how her best friend and housemate Lynne reacted to her marriage:

"My marriage had a tremendous impact on Lynne. It took her several years to adjust. Before I married, we had done everything together. We lived together, we ate together, we exercised together, we even went to the same church. We were like sisters. My marriage came as a real blow to her. I just wasn't able to be there for her the way I had been before. I tried to be—as much as I could. There were times when I wanted to go back and be there for her in the same old way, but I knew I couldn't without undermining my marriage. Lynne grieved the passing of that phase of our friendship as she would have grieved a death. For her, it was a death."

When the passage into parenthood leaves one of the two friends behind, this too can cause strain in the friendship.

The new mother can hardly help but be consumed with the overwhelming joys and terrors of her new role. The childless friend suddenly finds her formerly fun soul mate boring beyond words. She has no desire to spend their precious moments together talking about the baby's latest feat. And if she desperately wants to have a child but is unable to bear one, she might find it too painful to be around children or talk of babies.

Divorce and widowhood also produce changes in friendships. So do changes involving employment. If you work with your friend, and one of you changes jobs, a change in your friendship will follow. Or if you and your friend have both stayed at home to raise your children and one of you takes a job outside the home, this can have a profound effect on your friendship.

A Change in Values

More subtle but equally as problematic is a change in values. Frances recounted with sadness the change in her friendship with Maxine when Maxine adopted a strong anti-Halloween stance:

"I didn't even send my children out trick-or-treating. But I didn't want to turn the trick-or-treaters away from my door. I went out and bought a whole bunch of Halloween tracts to give out to the kids along with candy, but so many kids came this year, that eventually we ran out of the tracts. When Maxine heard that I had given out candy without tracts, she accused me of participating in the devil's holiday. She has been giving me the cold shoulder ever since."

In this case, the issue of Halloween became more important to Maxine than the friendship. Their views differed slightly on how to celebrate this holiday, but the fundamental change was in how much Maxine valued the friendship.

Paula and Shawn were best friends and prayer partners for many years. They were able to talk about anything and everything, spiritual, personal, and otherwise. They attended the same church and worked side by side in ministry. Shawn encouraged Paula when Paula suffered wounds inflicted by several rather insensitive members of the church. Shawn grew anxious as she watched Paula become disenchanted with the church. Paula dropped out of ministry, and her attendance became sporadic. Finally, she left the church altogether. Despite Paula's distance from the church (and presumably from God), Shawn still cared deeply about her dear friend. She wanted to retain the friendship. But many of the things they used to talk about now caused Paula great discomfort. Paula no longer valued prayer and Bible study, ministry, and a close walk with God. Often Shawn felt tongue-tied in her presence.

Change is rarely welcome in true friendship. When we have a good thing going, the last thing we want is to have it threatened. Because transitions upset the dynamic of a friendship, we find them threatening.

Yet, in this life, change is inevitable. God moves people in and out of our spheres of daily life. He allows changes in our friends' circumstances, attitudes, values, and relationships. Each day brings a fresh unfolding of God's eternal purposes. We must determine how we will respond to the changes that God brings with each unfolding.

Responses to Transitions

Refuse to Accept the Change

One possible response to transition is to refuse to accept the change. I do not recommend this response. To refuse to accept change is to deny the truth. If we say, "Your move won't change our friendship," then we are only fooling ourself. The friendship cannot help but change when the context and frequency of the contacts are radically altered.

When we refuse to accept changes that God has allowed in our lives by his sovereign power and grace, then we plug our ears and don blinders for our eyes. Thus we close ourselves off from learning new lessons, growing in faith, and seeing new opportunities that God may be sending our way. We are so adamant about having our own way and protecting our territory—the friendship that we so treasure—that we forget that friendship is a gift. It cannot be seized and held like booty.

Ultimately, this attitude will destroy the friendship. Friendships cannot stay healthy and growing when they are being clutched at out of selfishness, fear, and disregard for God's leading.

Adapt to the Change

A second possible response to transition is to adapt to the change. This means different things for different types of transitions. How do we begin to adapt to unwanted or difficult changes in our friendships?

ACCEPT THE CHANGE

The often-quoted serenity prayer says, "God, give us grace to accept with serenity the things that cannot be changed, courage to change the things that should be changed, and the wisdom to distinguish the one from the other." Most of these transitions are outside our control. The sooner we accept the transition with serenity, the better off we'll be. We will still grieve. We will still have moments of intense pain when we want more than anything else to recapture the friendship the way it was before the change. Yet, if our lives are yielded to God, we are assured that all our circumstances, good and bad, pleasant and painful, are a part of his grand design for our lives. This we must accept by faith, trusting in God's power and goodness.

Expend Effort

When our friendship goes through a major change, we may have to expend more effort to make the friendship work. This may involve writing letters, traveling to see each other, initiating special get-togethers.

Mary Jane is in her seventies. She told me the story of her four lifelong friends and how much they mean to each other.

Three out of the five friends were born within one or two days of each other at the same hospital. Their mothers had adjacent rooms. They were friends as they grew up together, attending the same school. During their high school years, Mary Jane asked her mother if she and her friends could use their garage-loft apartment for Friday night sleep overs. Her mother agreed under two conditions: that they always went in and out through the house, letting her know when they came in and left, and that there were no boys allowed. The girls followed these rules. Every Friday night for four years, the girls spent the night in the apartment, talking and laughing.

Marriage and children intervened, yet still the five friends kept in touch. Twice a year they got together (and still do) for the weekend. The first night of their weekend together, they each have twenty minutes to share uninterrupted the highlights of their lives since they were last together. When the twenty-minute time limit is up, the rest of the group interrupts and moves on to the next person. That way everyone has her turn. After that, conversation is a free-for-all, and by the end of the weekend, everyone has shared everything she wanted to share.

Several years ago, one of the five friends died of a brain tumor. "I can't believe one of us is gone!" Mary Jane said to the others when they gathered for the first time after the funeral. Later, the departed friend's daughter was married. The four remaining friends all attended the wedding and sat in the front row in her mother's place.

When Mary Jane's husband died, her mother said, "Honey, husbands come and husbands go. Children grow up and leave to live their own lives. But your women friends will always be there. Nurture those friendships."

I certainly recommend nurturing our marriages first and foremost, yet Mary Jane's mother had a point. In many cases, our women friends will outlive our husbands. Because Mary Jane and her friends made the effort to keep in touch, their friendships have endured throughout the years.

EXTEND GRACE

We may have high expectations for our friendship, envisioning frequent letter writing and regular visits in the case of a move. Our friend, however, may desire this level of correspondence and contact, but it may be completely outside her capabilities to maintain it.

Even friends in the same town can lose touch when lifestyle changes prevent regular contact. Now that my children are almost grown and I am busy with my career, I rarely see Linda, who homeschools her two older children while caring for the two younger ones. Our lives are on different tracks.

Recently I realized with shame that I had allowed months to elapse without calling Linda. I began our long-overdue telephone conversation with an apology: "I'm so sorry I haven't called you, Linda!"

"Ann, don't worry about it," Linda hastened to assure me. "I don't have any expectations at all. Whenever we are able to talk or get together, I treasure it as a wonderful gift."

Linda extended grace by releasing me from any sense of obligation. She conveyed to me that I need not feel guilty when I get so caught up in the immediate pressures of life that I neglect our friendship. Our relationship no longer depends on regular, frequent contact. It is firmly based on something far more eternal. Linda's words reminded me of this and expressed to me God's grace.

Extending grace means loving our friend without reprisal when she fails to put as much into the friendship as we wish she would. It means remaining sensitive to the pressures she is under and responding in such a way as to relieve pressure rather than intensify it. It means giving her slack when she needs it and continuing to believe the best about her.

GIVE FREEDOM

Sometimes our friend has moved beyond her need of our friendship, or she has moved into a new realm of life or ministry where we cannot follow. If we love her, we must respond by giving her freedom. We must not try to hold her back in order to fulfill our own friendship needs. Rather, we must allow her to go her way with our heartfelt blessing. This brings me to the final response to transitions: relinquishment.

Relinquish the Friendship

The third way of responding to transitions is to relinquish the friendship. We give it up. We hold our friendship in the palm of an open hand, willing at any moment to let it fly away. For those who are deeply committed to friendships, this is very difficult. Here the challenge is to trust God and accept his will, even when it means the loss of a treasured friendship. For those who move on to new horizons readily without looking back, the challenge is to make sure that this is true relinquishment and not mere laziness. Perhaps God wants you to grow in the area of commitment to your friendships.

One final word about adapting to change in friendship: Adaptation should never encompass compromise of our principles in matters of integrity and biblical morality.

When continuing in a friendship necessitates participation in wrong behavior, we must cut off the friendship.

When Change Is Needed

Thus far we have looked at scenarios in which we are the responders. The change happens, and we must decide how we will deal with that change. What about when we see that change is needed in the friendship? When and how should we take the initiative in instigating change in the friendship?

Something in the Friendship Makes Us Uncomfortable

Sometimes a friend, even a true friend, will begin to encroach on our personal space. Our friend takes liberties that violate our "house rules" or our own preferences. Take the situation of the drop-in friend. I love when friends stop by unannounced. That way, I haven't had to clean my house. I can enjoy their company without any expectations of "entertaining." Being a rather spontaneous sort, I also like to stop by friends' houses if I happen to be in the neighborhood and have a few extra minutes. My only expectation is a chance to catch up face to face if my friend is available.

This drives many women crazy. Some women consider stopping by unannounced the height of rudeness. Others simply are planners by nature and don't do well with surprises in their day. There is absolutely nothing wrong with this approach to life. God designed them this way. Their preferences and comfort zones are a part of their own unique identity, just as my spontaneity is part of what makes me the person I am.

This is a rather benign example. Other situations are more sensitive. Your friend may be getting too friendly with your husband. Or you may feel that she is taking advantage of you. You are beginning to feel she values you more for what you do for her than for who you are. Your friend may call at times when your family needs your attention—or when you need your sleep! Or your friend may be calling more frequently than you want, demanding more time than you feel you should give to this friendship. She may be borrowing money and forgetting to repay you.

All of these situations call for setting boundaries. We set boundaries when we draw a line and tell our friend, "You may come this far and no farther." In the case of the drop-in friend, the planner might say, "I love being with you, but you know, I'm a planner, and I have a hard time with spontaneous drop-by company. I really want to get together with you, though. Could we either set a regular time to do it or else just give each other a call to arrange it ahead of time? I know I'm probably a little compulsive, but that's what I'm comfortable doing."

We set boundaries by communicating, "This is what I need," in a way that is sensitive and loving, but firm. Whenever we set a boundary in a friendship (or any relationship), we risk resistance from the other person. The reason is simple. Unless we are in pain, we usually resist change with every fiber of our being. If our friend likes the arrangement as it is, she has no motivation to make a change in the relationship. When this is the case, we need to be prepared for our friend to do whatever she can to change things back to the way they were.

We also face internal resistance. We feel selfish insisting on our own way in a certain area. But if our boundary is in the interest of the friendship, or in our friend's best interest, or in obedience to God's leading in our life, then we must stand firm. This may disappoint our friend (although often such disappointment is temporary). She may have had other expectations of us and of our friendship.

However, God has not called us to live up to everyone else's expectations. Jesus was called everything in the book when he refused to fit in with others' plans for him, including the plans of his closest friends. First and foremost, Jesus was in communion with his heavenly Father. Out of this relationship and the guidance he received, Jesus set the pace for his own life. He did not allow others to manipulate him.

We need simply to make the changes we feel compelled to make. At the same time, we must recognize that these changes will produce anxiety in our friend. So we must be careful to assure her of our continued love and commitment to the friendship.

The Friendship Becomes Unhealthy

There are times, however, when we find that it is necessary to withdraw from the friendship altogether. This is the case when the friendship ceases to be mutually beneficial. Something in the friendship is unhealthy, and addressing the problem doesn't help.

Tara reached this conclusion about her friendship with Joyce. Tara truly loved Joyce and wanted more than anything to encourage her and help her grow spiritually and personally. No matter what Tara did, Joyce became more and more attached to her, mimicking her every move. After many years of praying for Joyce and spending time with her, Tara saw that for whatever reason, this friendship was not really helping Joyce. Furthermore, it was becoming exceedingly burdensome to Tara.

Tara began to set some boundaries. When Joyce asked for advice, Tara no longer counseled her. Tara stopped initiating get-togethers, and when Joyce initiated, Tara didn't drop everything to be with her. Joyce began to spend more time with other people as a result. In this manner, the friendship naturally diminished. When Joyce moved out of the area, she made no attempt to keep in touch with Tara.

In a sense, Joyce ultimately made the choice to terminate the friendship when she no longer gleaned what she needed from the relationship. It was Tara's responsibility, however, to stop propping up a relationship that had become detrimental to Joyce. Tara knew she had become a hindrance to Joyce because she had become the focus of Joyce's life.

During the period when Tara was making changes in how she interacted with Joyce, she had one direct conversation with her in which she said, "Joyce, my intention was never to lead you to me. You don't need me. You need the Lord." This was a hard conversation because Tara did not want Joyce to feel rejected. She wanted to communicate that she loved her, but the friendship was no longer helpful to either of them. She decided against saying too much, lest her words cause Joyce even more hurt. She remembered Proverbs 10:19, which says, "When words are many, sin is not absent."

This is an excellent principle to keep in mind when we face difficult transitions in our friendships. So often we use many words to cover up our own insecurities. We want to smooth things over or present ourselves as being beyond reproach. Much better to get to the point with simple words that are both loving and truthful. And often it is better to say nothing at all.

When do we decide to let a friendship go? And when do we work extra hard to maintain a friendship through passages that cause strain and separation? The only place to find the answers to these questions is on our knees. If God is at work in and through our friendship, then we are seeing mutual enrichment. And if he desires to continue to use our friendship to encourage us, we must be willing to make the necessary adaptations. On the other hand, the transition may be God's way of saying, "Let this one go. I have other friendships, other work for you to do."

We can only determine which course to take by seeking God. He has a purpose for all our friendships. Through all the ups and downs of true friendship, through transitions, through encouragement, through accountability, through disappointment, his purpose is to transform us. He is at work in our friendships so that we may be "transformed into his likeness with ever-increasing glory" (2 Cor. 3:18).

Questions for Personal Reflection

1. How have transitions affected your close friendships? Is there a "lost" friendship that you wish to reclaim?

2. How do we know when to expend more effort to maintain a friendship and when simply to relinquish the friendship?

3. Think of boundaries that you need to set in some of your friendships. Consider how to communicate this lovingly so that you do not hurt your friends.

*The only gift is a portion
of thyself.*

Ralph Waldo Emerson

12 The Gift That Transforms

Two weeks from the time of this writing, I will celebrate my fortieth birthday. As I consider how I will observe this momentous occasion, I think about my friends. I want to surround myself with the friends whose love has shaped my life.

Many of my closest friendships have spanned the entire length of my adult years. They have endured many transitions, their bond strengthening over time. As I reflect on the past eighteen years, I recall all the big milestones and how my friends were there for me. I remember their milestones as well.

I sprang the news to Linda that I was expecting my first child by flinging open my door and proudly displaying a maternity tee shirt with the word *BABY* embroidered across the front. Linda's excitement rivaled my own. After Mark's birth, Linda sneaked onto the maternity ward during nonvisiting hours because she couldn't wait to see me and the baby. Another milestone occurred on a lovely evening one June. I sat in the audience bursting with pride as Linda accepted her cap and her diploma. My dear friend was now a registered nurse! Several years later, Linda stayed with our children while Jim and I took a week-long second honeymoon at Linda's urging. When Linda married Michael, I was one of her attendants. It was an emotional day for me. I was thrilled for her, yet I wondered if I might be losing a part of myself. After that came baby showers and darling children one after another. Linda was in and out of the hospital so quickly when she delivered her babies that I had to visit her at home.

Debbie also figures into the milestones and memories from those years. Debbie and her husband, John, cared for nineteen-month-old Mark when I was in the hospital delivering Laura. Debbie retrieved me in her old, beat-up car without shock absorbers. That ride home from the hospital was an uncomfortable one after my cesarean section! Several years we traipsed out to Christmas tree farms together to cut our own trees, including the year Debbie was due to give birth to her first child. Our photo albums are filled with pictures of the Hibbards and the Bennetches—Christmas celebrations, birthdays, camping trips. The early years were marked by home improvement projects our husbands worked on together while Debbie and I visited and prepared food. We took care of each other's children and cheered each other on in the challenge of parenting. A year ago I stood beside Debbie at her mother's graveside.

Linda and Debbie are two precious friends whose lives are woven together with mine. These women have had a tremendous impact on me. The constancy of their love anchored my heart when circumstances, temptation, and pressures threatened shipwreck. When my career aspirations began to consume me, they gently reminded me of my priorities. When I felt like a failure as a wife or mother and wanted to throw in the towel, their prayers and support lifted me up and helped me persevere.

Treasured Friends

These friends know me inside and out. They know my family, my history, my strengths and weaknesses, my past mistakes, my idiosyncrasies. And still they love me! What an overwhelming thought!

Because of their love, I am transformed. Built up by their confidence in me, I have courage to attempt daring endeavors. I am more sensitive to others' pain because I have walked with my friends through their dark valleys. My family relationships are stronger as a result of my friends' encouragement and accountability. Knowing that they believe in me prompts me to keep striving for what is true and good. Knowing that they accept me no matter what enables me to accept my failures, learn from them, and work to do better.

I am so grateful for the friends that God has brought into my life. Day by day he uses them to change me. The changes are often imperceptible in the short run, but in the long run, they are undeniable.

Because true friendship touches us in the deepest part of our being, it has the power to change us—radically and irrevocably. Love always transforms the beloved, and a true friendship filled with love cannot help but change the lives of both friends.

Love makes us bold. We think, *My friend thinks I'm terrific. So for right now, I'll take her word for it. Instead of having to protect myself, now I can look at some things in myself that I was afraid to look at before. With my friend holding my hand, I can step out in faith. With her by my side, encouraging me, I can make some changes.*

True Friendship Teaches Us to Love

True friendship teaches us to love. We cannot learn how to love by sitting alone at home reading a book or by contemplating on a mountaintop. Love is learned in the crucible of human relationships: a place where we bind each other's wounds, clothe each other with honor, nourish each other with encouragement, and quench each other's thirst for acceptance and companionship.

In true friendship, we learn to give of ourselves. We spend time with our friend, time that does not advance our careers, make us money, look good on our résumés, or gain us position in the community. We simply give of our time because we love our friend and want to be with her.

And when our friend is in great need, true friendship compels us to give of ourselves in extraordinary measure. It may be inconvenient, expensive, and emotionally draining, but we pay the price that love demands. Love is costly.

Jesus said, "For whoever wants to save his life will lose it, but whoever loses his life for me will save it. What good is it for a man to gain the whole world, and yet lose or forfeit his very self?" (Luke 9:24–25). When we give of ourselves for our friend, we serve Christ himself. In losing our lives, we save our lives because we reap the immeasurable blessings of love.

We learn by experience that love doesn't run out; it multiplies. We discover that the joy of giving far outweighs the pleasures of self-indulgence. And with time, we see that giving of ourselves in love ignites a chain reaction of good in the lives of many individuals. Every time we learn one of these lessons in giving, we are strengthened in our motivation and ability to love again and again and again. Thus we are transformed.

In true friendship, we learn the humility of receiving. This is perhaps the harder of the two lessons of love. We must learn to lay aside our illusions of self-sufficiency. Our pride tells us that we are perfectly capable of handling life on our own. True friendship teaches us to lean on our friend, not in dependency but in mutual support.

Let's face it, there are times when each of us is not very lovable. We all have an ugly side. A true friend sees our ugliness and gives us forgiveness, acceptance, and continued love. "How difficult it is to receive, and to go on receiving, from others a love that does not depend on our own attraction," wrote C. S. Lewis in *The Four Loves*.[1] This is a humbling process that occurs only in the most intimate of relationships. It is a picture of God's grace, his abundance lavished on undeserving sinners. And God uses the medium of friendship to teach us lessons about grace.

True Friendship Makes Us More like Jesus

As we learn to love, we become more and more like Jesus. In Paul's prayer for the Ephesians, recorded in Ephesians 3:16–19, we read,

> I pray that out of his glorious riches he may strengthen you with power through his Spirit in your inner being, so that Christ may dwell in your hearts through faith. And I pray that you, being rooted and established in love, may have power, together with all the saints, to grasp how wide and long and high and deep is the love of Christ, and to know this love that surpasses knowledge—that you may be filled to the measure of all the fullness of God.

The goal is to be filled to the measure of all the fullness of God, to be like Jesus, "the image of the invisible God" (Col. 1:15). Our friendships in Christ are a part of God's means for accomplishing that goal in our lives, as noted by the references above to "love" and "together with all the saints." Along with other means, including trials, teaching from his Word, and family relationships, God uses true friendships to mold and shape our character. How does he do this? God shows us Jesus in our friend and makes us want to be like him.

True friends value one another. We see qualities in one another that we appreciate and admire. Anything that is honorable and praiseworthy comes from God. We see in our friend aspects of the character of God, and we are drawn to these qualities because our hearts long for God himself.

C. S. Lewis wrote,

> Friendship . . . is the instrument by which God reveals to each the beauties of all the others. They are no greater than the beauties of a thousand other men; by Friendship God opens our eyes to them. They are, like all beauties, derived from Him, and then, in a good Friendship, increased by Him through the Friendship itself, so that it is His instrument for creating as well as for revealing. At this feast it is He who has spread the board and it is He who has chosen the guests. It is He, we may dare to hope, who sometimes does, and always should, preside. Let us not reckon without our Host.[2]

We see the beauty of Jesus Christ in our friend, and that causes us to change. Like a plant growing in the direction of the sunlight, we begin to grow in the direction of God's sunlight, as shone forth in the character of our friend.

The following poem by an unknown author expresses beautifully this process at work in true friendship.

A Glimpse of Him

Not only by the words we say
Not only by our deeds confessed,
But in a most unconscious way
Is Christ expressed.

For me, 'twas not the truth you taught
To you, so clear, to me, so dim,
But when you came to me
You brought a glimpse of him.

And from your eyes, he beckoned me,
And from your heart, his love was shed,
'Til I lost sight of you
And saw the Christ instead.

To desire to have this effect on our friends is a worthy goal. The problem is that the moment it becomes a conscious thought on our part, we lose the ability to impart Christ's likeness, for we are looking at ourselves. The secret lies in losing ourselves completely in our love of Jesus Christ. God uses us best when we are least conscious of it. Oswald Chambers wrote, "When a little child becomes conscious of being a little child, the child-likeness is gone; and when a saint becomes conscious of being a saint, something has gone wrong."[3]

True Friendship Makes Us Long for Heaven

As long as we are in this world, however, sin continues to plague us. We cannot entirely break free from self-centeredness, pride, and fear, sins that encumber all our relationships. Sin causes misunderstanding between friends. Sin causes divisions that sever true friendships. We grapple with our grief over these painful losses, and we long for heaven, where there will be no more sin.

How wonderful it will be to enjoy friendships that bear no taint of jealousy, no hint of self-interest, no trace of hurt feelings. In heaven, we will for the first time understand True Friendship. All our friendships there will be perfect replicas of the friendship between the three persons of the Trinity. We will bask in the multicolored light of the full spectrum of God's love.

Revelation 21:4 tells us that in heaven "He will wipe every tear from their eyes. There will be no more death or mourning or crying or pain, for the old order of things has passed away." We mourn our lost friendships when circumstances, distance, or death part us. We long for heaven, where there will be no more separation.

With the passage of time, one by one God takes our Christian friends home to be with him. Elderly friends tell me how most of their loved ones wait for them on the other side of death. They yearn to be reunited with friends whom they haven't seen for many years.

But we must be careful, lest our desire for our friendships overtake our true heavenly prize—God himself. Saint Augustine wrote, "Thou hast made us for thyself, and our heart has no rest till it comes to Thee." In heaven, we will come face to face with perfect love. We will know true friendship unlike anything we have experienced on earth.

Lewis writes,

> In heaven, there will be no anguish and no duty of turning away from our earthly Beloveds. First, because we shall have turned already; from the portraits to the Original, from the rivulets to the Fountain, from the creatures He made lovable to Love Himself. But secondly, because we shall find them all in Him. By loving Him more than them we shall love them more than we now do.[4]

We long for heaven, where we will know the one true love from whom all true friendships flow. All that we enjoy of true friendship here on earth will be ours in much greater measure in our eternal friendship with Jesus Christ. All that we wish for in a friend is embodied in him. Every taste of joy in true friendship here on earth is but a teaser to whet our appetites for the great banquet that awaits us.

Questions for Personal Reflection

1. How have your true friendships transformed your life?

2. If you were to present each of your friends with an award for what her friendship has given you, what would that award be?

3. What qualities of Christlikeness shine forth from each of your friends? Write them notes expressing these thoughts.

Discussion Questions

Chapter 1: True Friends

1. Based on your own experience, how would you answer the question What is a true friend?
2. Ann lists three common elements in true friendship: self-revelation, support, and service. How does each of these contribute to true friendship?
3. What do you think of the idea of a trust circle in regard to friendship? When have you experienced this kind of support?
4. Read the three Gospel accounts of Jesus' prayer in Gethsemane: Matthew 26:36–46; Mark 14:31–42; and Luke 22:39–46. Describe Jesus' emotional state. How does he show his need for his friends?
5. Why do you think Jesus withdrew from his friends to pray alone?
6. Read John 15:13. What does this verse mean to you in your relationship with Jesus? In your relationship with your friends?
7. What do you hope to learn about true friendship from this study? Let's pray together that God will teach each of us what he would have us learn.

Chapter 2: For Everything a Season

1. Can you recall extended periods of time when you have had to wait for a true friend? Describe your thoughts and feelings during that time.

2. Read James 1:17. How does this apply to true friendship? How can waiting be a gift?
3. Can you think of a time when you prayed for a friend and God provided one?
4. Read John 15:16. What does this tell us about Jesus' approach to friendship?
5. Do you find it easy or difficult to take the initiative with a potential friend? What helps you take that first step?
6. When do you think it is okay to stop trying to make a friendship work and "move on"?
7. Do you think it is important to examine yourself and your relationships? Why or why not?

Chapter 3: The Balancing Act

1. What is it about your season of life that makes it difficult (or easy) to find time for friendship?
2. Read Romans 8:28 and Psalm 145:14–19. How do these passages apply to your current time pressures and your desires for true friendship?
3. How do you think God views our overly busy schedules? Read Psalm 46:10.
4. Why do we overcrowd our schedules so that we don't have time for friendship with God or others?
5. What activities in your life could you creatively combine with friendship? (Think about activities such as exercise, work, hobbies, ministry, prayer . . .)
6. Look at Mark 9:2–8 and John 21:15–22. Reflect on Jesus' example of focusing on a few. How might you apply this principle to your friendships?
7. Are there any changes you feel God would have you make in your schedule or your approach to friendships after reading this chapter?

Chapter 4: A Safe Haven

1. Read Colossians 3:12. How do these qualities help build trust in a friendship?
2. How would you define authenticity? What difference does this make in developing a true friendship?
3. Read Romans 12:15. How does this verse apply to a true friendship?

4. Read Psalm 20:1, 4–5. How is this an example of positive empathy?
5. What safety hazards crop up in your friendships? What can you do about them?
6. Read Ephesians 4:29. How does this principle apply to the problems of jealousy, gossip, and breaking a confidence?
7. Read Hebrews 4:15–16 and Matthew 11:28–30. Why are we safe with Jesus? How can Jesus' example help us in our friendships?

Chapter 5: A Listening Ear

1. What bad habits prevent you from being a good listener?
2. What attitudes underlie these habits?
3. What new attitudes should you adopt in order to become a better listener and a better friend?
4. How do these new attitudes translate into new behaviors?
5. Read the excerpt from Dietrich Bonhoeffer's *Life Together* on pp. 85–86. Do you think his words, written more than half a century ago, apply to Christians today? Why or why not?
6. What changes do you desire to make in your attitudes and behaviors regarding listening?
7. Meditate on Philippians 2:3–8. How does this apply to the subject of listening to one's friend?

Chapter 6: The Strong Arms of a Friend

1. Tell about a friend who demonstrated extraordinary love when you were in need. What did you find especially helpful?
2. Read 1 John 3:18. What does this verse mean to you in the arena of friendship?
3. Read John 15:13. What specific aspects of our lives must we lay down when we serve a friend in need?
4. What are your God-given limitations?
5. Do you need to learn to live within your limitations or do you need to extend yourself more for your friends? How can you go about making these changes?
6. Read the story of the good Samaritan in Luke 10:25–37. What was Jesus trying to convey?

7. How do you determine when to help and when to refrain from helping? What bearing does 2 Peter 1:3 have on this problem?

Chapter 7: The Power of Encouragement

1. Can you think of an instance when the encouragement of a friend had a significant impact on your life?
2. Read Ecclesiastes 4:9–12. How do these verses depict encouragement?
3. How does laughter give encouragement? Can you think of any examples from your life?
4. When do you need encouragement simply by a friend's presence? Why is this so important?
5. What is *synergism*? How does this term relate to encouragement in true friendship?
6. How can we encourage our friends with words of truth without sounding as if we have all the answers?
7. What role does prayer play in encouraging our friends?
8. Read Hebrews 3:13. How does encouragement keep us from becoming hardened by sin's deceitfulness?

Chapter 8: Going against the Grain

1. How do you respond to differences between people? How have these reactions affected your friendships?
2. Read 1 John 4:18. How does this verse apply to dealing with differences in your friendships?
3. What is it that you fear when you find yourself avoiding areas of potential conflict?
4. How do you determine when parting ways is the right response to a difference?
5. Read Romans 5:8; 15:7. What do these verses tell us about Christ's acceptance of us? What implications does this have for our responses to our friends when differences surface?
6. Read the love chapter, 1 Corinthians 13. How do these qualities apply to dealing with differences in friendship? In light of this, what changes might you need to make in the way you handle differences?

Chapter 9: Tough Love

1. Describe a mutually accountable friendship in your life. What makes it work? If you do not have one, why do you think this is absent in your friendships?
2. What do you find difficult about accountability?
3. Consider James 5:16. How can mutual confession bring healing?
4. Read Proverbs 12:1; 15:31. How do these verses apply to friendship?
5. Read Matthew 5:23–24. What does this tell us about the importance Jesus placed on reconciled relationships?
6. Read Matthew 18:15–17. What pattern does Jesus give us for dealing with an offense? How can this work in our friendships?
7. Under what circumstances should you confront a friend? How should you proceed?

Chapter 10: The Sting of Disappointment

1. Have you been disappointed in a friendship? What are your thoughts and feelings about that situation today?
2. Read Ephesians 4:2. What are some current issues in your friendships about which you need to "bear with [your friend] in love"?
3. What are the four A's of a complete apology? Why is each of these components important?
4. Read Matthew 18:21–35. What lesson does this parable teach us?
5. Consider Lewis Smedes's words, "When we forgive, we set a prisoner free and discover that the prisoner we set free is us." How have you found this to be true in your experience?
6. Why is forgiveness "the most unnatural act a person can perform"?
7. What does "forgiving one another as Christ forgave you" mean in your experience?

Chapter 11: The Sands of Time

1. How have transitions affected your close friendships? Is there a "lost" friendship that you wish to reclaim?
2. What kind of transitions do you find most difficult?
3. How do you usually deal with transitions?

4. How do you know when to expend more effort to maintain a friendship and when simply to relinquish the friendship?
5. Think of boundaries you need to set in some of your friendships. How can you communicate this lovingly so that you do not hurt your friends?
6. Consider the transitions the disciples faced in their relationship with Jesus during his death, resurrection, and ascension. What emotions do you suppose they experienced?
7. Read Matthew 28:16–20. How might Jesus' words have helped them with this final transition? What lessons can we learn from this?

Chapter 12: The Gift That Transforms

1. Read Luke 9:24–25. How does this verse apply to true friendship?
2. How does true friendship teach us to love?
3. How does God use true friendship to make us more like his Son?
4. How does true friendship make us long for heaven?
5. How have true friendships transformed your life?
6. What differences have this book and this study made in your approach to friendship?
7. Read aloud together the poem "A Glimpse of Him" on pp. 194–95. Join in a time of prayer and thanksgiving for the gift of true friendship.

Notes

Chapter 5: A Listening Ear

1. Dietrich Bonhoeffer, *Life Together*, trans. John W. Doberstein (New York: Harper & Brothers, 1954), 97–99.

Chapter 7: The Power of Encouragement

1. O. Hallesby, *Prayer* (Minneapolis: Augsburg, 1975), 80–81.

Chapter 9: Tough Love

1. The persons described in this story are composites and do not represent any one specific person. Their conversations and problems represent situations I have encountered numerous times in counseling with women across the country.

Chapter 10: The Sting of Disappointment

1. The persons described in this story are composites and do not represent any one specific person. Their conversations and problems represent situations I have encountered numerous times in counseling with women across the country.

2. LaVonne Neff, ed., *Breakfast with the Saints: 120 Readings from Great Christians* (Ann Arbor, Mich.: Servant Publications, 1996), 101.

3. Lewis B. Smedes, *The Art of Forgiving: When You Need to Forgive and Don't Know How* (Nashville: Moorings, 1996), 178.

4. Francis A. Schaeffer, *The Mark of the Christian* (Downers Grove, Ill.: InterVarsity Press, 1970), 24–25.

5. Smedes, *Art of Forgiving*, 92.

6. Ibid., 93–94.

7. This quote appears on the jacket of *The Art of Forgiving* by Lewis Smedes.

8. Sister Helen Prejean, *Dead Man Walking* (New York: Random House, 1993), 244.

Chapter 12: The Gift That Transforms

1. C. S. Lewis, *The Four Loves* (New York: Harcourt Brace Jovanovich, 1960), 182.

2. Ibid., 126–27.

3. Oswald Chambers, *Our Brilliant Heritage*, quoted in *Christianity Today*, 15 May 1995, 36.

4. Lewis, *Four Loves*, 191.